Sabotage

The nasty little secret we all know holds us back!

MIKE CONNAWAY

Tulsa, Oklahoma

SABOTAGE—THE NASTY LITTLE SECRET WE ALL KNOW HOLDS US BACK!

Sabotage—The Nasty Little Secret We All Know Holds Us Back!
by Mike Connaway
Published by Insight Publishing Group
8801 S. Yale, Suite 410
Tulsa, OK 74137
918-493-1718

ISBN 1-930027-81-8

Library of Congress catalog card number: 2003105067

Printed in the United States of America

DEDICATION

To Lisa, my wife of twenty years—Thank you for still being interested in my ideas. You have seen all my dirty laundry and still brag about me to everyone you meet. Wow!

A special thanks to Jim Folger—my best friend and personal coach. It's hard to find people who do so much to help you win and enjoy watching you receive the trophy. You are an example of a person with great self-esteem.

Table of Contents

FOREWORD

by Coach Fred Akers

Coach Mike is at the top of his game when he is teaching all of us how to become high performance people. His amazing insight into the human mind and its impact on success, combined with his uncanny ability to communicate his message in a way that makes us all say, "I can do that!" is what won me over as a Coach Mike fan.

I've played and coached sports at the highest level, been head coach of the football program at UT, had 23 bowl game appearances, and had players go on to succeed in the NFL. In all of this, I've learned a lot about spotting talent and knowing what it takes to coach people into their potential.

With that said, Coach Mike is a one-in-a-million talent find, but more importantly, he knows how to unlock the talents and potential in others. If I were you, I'd join his team right away!

Coach Fred Akers
CEO, Akers Performance Group
Former head football coach: University of Texas

Dad and I have had the opportunity to work with many of the great leaders in the world, from some of the top business CEOs and military generals to the movers and shakers in the political world. We've also had the great privilege of brainstorming with Coach Mike on numerous occasions—*and his insights have many times made the difference for us!*

He is a true champion in the world of mind-set. What you will get from Coach Mike is never regurgitated motivational hype, but rather something that is always cutting edge and extremely fresh. If you read his materials, watch his videos, listen to his CDs, or have the chance to meet him in person, I am confident you will say the same thing I tell people about Mike: "When I get around Coach Mike, I always feel bigger."

Dan Akers,
President, Akers Performance Group

Here's What Other Leaders Are Saying About *Sabotage* and Author, Mike Connaway

Sabotage is a book that everyone in my company will read at least twice! I'm not a person who likes hype. Give me tools and I can build anything. This book is just that—real mind-set tools that take the mind to the next level.

Daniel Anderson
CEO, Stratia Corporation

"Mike Connaway is "the" new millennium coach. A fresh and extremely talented coach, who exudes the rare attributes of servant leadership the world so desperately needs. His motivation, inspiration, presence, forward thinking, blended with his uncanny humor, will guide you to newer heights of personal power, wealth mind-set and life mastery. All who have been touched by Coach Mike, have been blessed in their quest for creating an extraordinary quality of life."

Dr. Michael Reid
CEO, Gorilla Chiropractic Coaching

Introduction

The phone rang. It was a woman in a particularly abusive situation asking for help. As part of a counseling team in one of the poorest neighborhoods in Seattle, it was my job to help

When we arrived, she thanked us profusely and told us how grateful she was for our coming. As she described the abuse she was receiving from her husband, we made the mistake of agreeing with her. By agreeing, we were stating that her husband was wrong, and she began to defend him!

Moments later, she drove us out of her apartment yelling and screaming at us calling us names I would not repeat to a sailor.

About face!

What would cause her to ask for help from her abuser, then turn around and defend him?

Logically it doesn't make sense, but psychologically it does. You see, our mind craves order and will go to great lengths to keep that order—even if that order is abusive! For this abused woman, she knows when she will be hit, when she will be yelled at, when she will be ignored, etc. Strangely, her mind clings to that order rather than embrace freedom.

And if she were somehow able to break free from her terrible situation, what would most likely happen to her? She would end up in the same type of situation. That is because she wants order more than she wants freedom.

Sabotage cycle

What does one woman's cycle of abuse have to do with you? ***Absolutely everything!***

Most people are on their own cycle, one that keeps them wishing for something better but never being able to attain it. So instead of looking down on this woman who couldn't seem to break out of her abusive situation, we need to ask ourselves, "Am I allowing my natural desire for order to keep me from reaching the next level of success?"

Most likely!

That is because we are quick to find ways to reject the new so that we can keep the old. We attack the opportunity or the person…and stay where we are. We do this constantly because reaching the next level of success will always cause us to give up our current order. But if we do somehow find success, we end up self-sabotaging and going right back to where we were, just like the abused woman.

> Are you allowing your natural desire for order to keep you from reaching the next level of success?

This is the very pattern that we need to break.

When this repeats for four or five generations, the odds of breaking free and moving up are virtually nonexistent. This means that unless you do something different, you will remain financially right where you are today.

Those are the facts, but your reality and these facts do not have to be the same. It might be difficult to break free of the situation you are in, but it's certainly not impossible. ***To get to the next level, you have to change—and that is the key to your freedom.***

Wisely, you are probably thinking, "Change is good, but where do I start?"

The place to start is the very place that demands you never change…your mind. It is the way you think that must be altered, for when you change your mind-set, everything else comes into place.

Part I

breaking out of the old

Chapter One

The mind-set of a millionaire —*foundation to fortune*

Taking charge of our destiny sounds great, but there is one thing to consider; you can never again blame someone else. Becoming a person of destiny means giving up the right to blame. What a wonderful way to live your life.

You were destined to fulfill your destiny. There is not a person on the planet or a circumstance you might face in life that has the right to interfere with your destiny! For most of us, however, the greatest interference does not come from some thing or some person; ***it comes from our own pattern of thinking***.

Breaking old patterns of thinking

We all have patterns of thinking. Our brief history—everything we have experienced to date—is stored in our mind, creating a pattern of thinking that will eventuate in beliefs that we cling to. These beliefs then dictate how we think, how we act, and what we do.

"But what if my pattern of thinking is wrong?" is a question that each of us must step back and honestly answer.

All thought patterns are set in stone, which is precisely why they call it a "mind-set." If our mind-set is wrong, then we will self-sabotage when it comes time to break out of our old thinking pattern and break into the new. ***In short, we are unable to reach our destiny because our mind would not allow it.***

Our mind wants order, thrives on order, and develops a pattern as quickly as possible to maintain that order. If something new comes along—whether good or bad—that takes us out of our pattern, our mind revolts and tries to take us back to what it considered "normal."

That is why, if you are middle class, the upper-class people don't want you to move up to their level and why the middle-class people don't want you to leave them behind. The mind-sets have been established and to even consider otherwise is mentally taboo. At the same time, your own middle-class mind-set is fighting against you!

> Ask yourself, "What if my pattern of thinking is wrong?"

To break out of the old pattern, you must understand how your mind operates, for only when you understand the process can you make it work to your benefit.

Understanding is everything

If you played a sport (for example, basketball) as a child, you might have been told by your coach, "You don't have what it takes to make the team—and you never will." That moment and those words stuck in your mind, so now when you hear the word "basketball" you instantly see yourself being downgraded by your old coach.

Attached to your very real picture are very real emotions. These emotions, interestingly enough, are not bound by time and are as real today as they were back then. The more vivid the picture in your mind, the higher priority it has, and the higher the priority, the more emotion that is attached to it.

From those emotions you form a belief system about yourself. In this case, the degrading experience was not a positive one and might very well be playing a self-sabotaging role in what you are doing, believing, and thinking today.

Or hopefully you had a coach who encouraged you with, "You can do it—I believe in you!" These words formed a picture with strong positive emotions that became part of your belief system that propelled you to success.

Either way, we all have the same pattern of thinking and it looks like this:

Words → Pictures → Emotions → Belief Systems

But how do you know your belief system is grounded on accurate information? Thomas Edison and Albert Einstein were both considered "stupid" or "slow" by some of their schoolteachers, but Edison and Einstein obviously didn't form their belief systems on those words! Examples of people who believed in themselves are endless, but even greater are the numbers of people who believed the negative words that were spoken about them.

To help make sure that you fulfill your destiny, it is important that you examine these two areas of your belief system:

#1—*Unchecked words.* Unchecked words lead to unchecked pictures that lead to unchecked emotions that eventuate in unchecked beliefs. This is where you act, think, and believe certain things without taking the time to find out if it's accurate. Beliefs that go unchecked are one of the surest ways to sabotage your financial future.

For example, there aren't any middle-class people who are satisfied where they are, but it isn't until they have a big need that they want to move to the next level. But because their minds have created order and a belief system about where they are, any advances to the next level are only temporary.

> Beliefs that go unchecked are one of the surest ways to sabotage your financial future.

Their belief system was built on words that went unchecked—and it sabotaged their success.

#2—*Moral walls.* Psychologists teach the four parts of a belief system, but I believe there is one more: moral walls. The complete pattern of thinking looks like this:

Words → Pictures→ Emotions→ Belief Systems → Moral Walls

These moral walls are built around beliefs as a protective wall. In time, the moral walls hold the belief system in place—and it is virtually impossible to change the beliefs because it has become a moral issue!

For example, I was at a conference with several wealthy businessmen when I heard an individual say that he hadn't been to church in twenty years. I didn't think much of it until the next day when I heard him say with passion that he took great offense at how people wore jeans to church.

I asked him, "You said you hadn't been to church in twenty years, why do you care how people dress?"

He paused…then said, "I really don't know."

At least he was honest, but how many of us have intense moral convictions that cannot be explained? The real question to answer is this: ***"Do I have moral walls keeping me from reaching the next level?"***

Foundation to fortune

It all comes back to your mind and the words that start your pattern of thinking. Part of rewriting the foundational words that dominate your thinking involves understanding your full potential.

Just for a minute, allow yourself to dream…you wake up tomorrow morning and every gift and talent you have and all your potential has come out at once. For the next full year, you are operating at 100 percent effectiveness. Imagine that!

Now, calculate what the dollar value would be for all your gifts and talents and abilities to be operating at 100 percent efficiency. What would that be worth? Be conservative. How much wealth would that produce?

> Our greatest challenge is our own pattern of thinking.

The average person says between $5 million and $20 million for that year. The number reflects you and your gifts—we aren't talking about someone else's gifts here. The gifts are yours. It was your true estimated value that you calculated.

With that number in mind, how do you feel about your potential now? This understanding of the value of your potential will help your vision for the future, ***but***

what you do will determine how much of your vision you truly believe you have a "right" to possess.

Do you believe you have the right to fulfill your potential? Many people don't think they deserve it or think they should not be rewarded. We must reset our foundations so that we are prepared for fortune, not failure.

4 areas that define you

Are you aware that you are being defined, programmed, and influenced by people and things on a daily basis? More likely than not, the defining and influencing you are receiving is not really what you want.

> If you think money is evil, then you will place a moral belief on your desire to gain more wealth—***and you won't gain more wealth.***

Here are the four areas that try to define you and how you can instead define yourself:

#1—your family

Your family is the #1 entity that seeks to define you. It affects you, your heritage, your personal family, your future, etc. Statistics show that if you are born on welfare you will most likely stay on welfare. That is simply because people seldom break out of the financial position they are born into. The truth is, your thinking defines who you are and what you believe about yourself.

To change your belief systems about yourself, you must reprogram how your family affects you. You are the only person who has the right to write your own future—not your mom, dad, brother, sister, or other family member. Their vision for you is not your own. You control your own destiny.

The fact that your family is trying to program you can be good or bad, but one fact remains—***your family is not going to help you to the next level!*** They won't understand and they might even take it personally, thinking you have rejected them. They have attached moral beliefs to their position, which is simply the result of their thought patterns. You have to give yourself the moral freedom to break the pattern of your family.

Here are three ways to break the negative thought patterns of your family:

1—***Remember that you are in charge of your destiny.*** Everything must be filtered through your destiny and purpose. If you don't write your own destiny and purpose, others will redefine it for you. No matter what people say, it doesn't matter—your purpose wins out. Understand that others either love you and your purpose or they don't really love you. Take control and take responsibility.

2—***Make sure that everyone in your family understands that you are a person of personal posture.*** Define yourself so that everyone sees you for who you are, no more and no less. If people like who you are, they can have more of you, your time, and your talents. If they don't like you, then respect them, but don't give them more of yourself. If you don't define yourself, someone else will always define you, and success will not be possible.

3—***Create an arena that allows people to come and go in your life.*** Don't take responsibility for people coming and going. If someone gets mad at you and they don't feel comfortable where you are going, feel free to say nicely, "I understand, but I'm not changing. If you want to join me, you are welcome to, but I'm moving on." If you think that you are serving them or loving them by staying behind, you are wrong. And if you give in to people, you will blame them and hate them, so give them the freedom to come and go—and love yourself enough to fulfill your destiny and purpose.

#2—the education system

Remember how a pattern of thinking begins with words? When you were in school, you received more words from your teachers than you did from your parents. That is normal, but the fact still holds true that whoever speaks into your life develops pictures that eventually lead to belief systems.

But did the people speaking into your life ***have what you wanted***? Teachers train us how to think, but what we learn in school is not going to make us successful, much less take us beyond the middle-class mentality.

In the late 1800s, almost everyone in the United States was an entrepreneur—94 percent were self-employed. But the Industrial Age changed everything. Assembly lines (for example, Henry Ford) and factory jobs became common, as did divorce. Before the Industrial Age, divorce was low, I believe, because people understood what it took to win together. Now we don't talk because we don't work together and we think we need a good job more than a spouse…and divorce rates skyrocketed.

> Until success is taught in school, success cannot be learned in school.

By the end of the 1900s, only 4 percent of Americans were self-employed! This Industrial Age mind-set defines us as a nation, but you can expand your thinking and ensure that you do not settle for the "accepted" status quo. Doing so will require an understanding of your thought patterns as well as a conscious effort to change those patterns.

Here are three principles to help transform your thinking:

1—*Continue to be a student.* Don't stop learning. Pick the information for yourself that challenges you. Choose something that keeps you growing. Learn about things that others must know who have the success you desire. Also, learn from those individuals directly. If what you read or are told makes you angry, fearful, etc., it's good for you! If you don't change, you won't grow.

For example, almost every book I've ever read on personal finances was different from what I was taught growing up. They brought an array of emotions like fear, anger and confusion; but I kept reading them anyway. I forced myself to be a student.

2—*Be grateful for mentors, but examine your own life.* If people who don't have what you want are trying to speak into your life, then be very careful to pick and choose their information. Don't swallow it all! Choose what only goes in line with your vision. Don't buy into their belief systems of what they think success really is. If they don't have what you are looking for, they probably don't have the information to get you there.

3—*Keep looking for more.* Treat the books you read and the information you are told as stepping-stones, not as final achievements of understanding. Keep looking for more. Ask yourself, "How does this affect my vision and how do I build upon this to make something productive out of it?" Take what you learn and move on.

#3—your finances

In regards to your finances, I believe we are all to be wealthy, but never should it be instant, quick, or easy. If it were, we would not be qualified to maintain it. Along the way toward becoming wealthy, there are three keys to unlocking your financial door:

#1—*Never turn money into a moral issue*. Have you ever said, "That athlete gets paid way too much"? To do so is to place your moral values on someone else. You are exposing how you think. The time will come when you can make more money than you make now, but you might self-sabotage because you made money a moral issue. Never make money a moral issue.

#2—*Never get emotionally attached to money*. Use it for what it's designed for. It's a tool. Don't get attached to it. Be emotionally stable and you'll be wiser, a smarter risk taker, etc. For example, see every home you buy as an investment. If you get too attached to it, that emotion will keep you bound.

#3—*Wherever there is a vision, there will be provision.* Keep yourself stirred up and focused on a vision. It will expand your abilities. Don't keep a moral commitment to your middle-class thinking. You may need to expand, get a bigger car, home, business, etc. Whatever your vision, increase your mind-set to get you there.

#4—the media

Whatever your desired area of success, the media plays a role. They aren't the enemy, but they have a clear social agenda. If you aren't clear on your own agenda, you may want to take a break from the media lest their agenda influence yours.

> Don't keep a moral commitment to your middle-class thinking.

Here are three reasons why:

#1—*The media is powerful*. The many voices, the exaggerations, and the inaccurate spins can impact you. Anything that grabs your focus can define who you are. Concerning money, there is an attitude in the media of demonizing the wealthy, as if being wealthy is evil. That mentality will affect how you think about yourself.

#2—*The media has an "it must be true if it's on TV" mentality.* The "godlike" quality of the media (it is in thousands of places at once and seems to have unlimited power) gives the perception that what is said must be true. If you aren't defined and clear in your own vision, then you will be refocused. You need to guard your mind-set from the pattern of thinking that is being given to you by the media.

#3—*There is an agenda by the media*. We all have agendas. Understand that your agenda won't be the same as the media. Highly successful people don't have time for someone else to define what is going on around them. They don't have time for someone else to define their reality. We need to do the same.

Now that you know what defines you, it is much easier to step back and redefine yourself. It all comes back to mind-set.

Most people you meet don't have the mind-set of a millionaire. You do, so be sure that the words, pictures, emotions, and beliefs you are building into your foundation are the ones that belong in the mind-set of a millionaire.

Chapter One

Steps to Success

- ❒ Most people are more in love with their own thoughts than they are their potential and destiny. If you're anything like me, you are going to have to divorce a few of those patterns that only served to sabotage your next level.

- ❒ Don't just work, understand how you work. The reason why I take lessons in golf is not just to learn to hit the ball better but also so I understand what's happening when things start going wrong.

- ❒ Calculate your value by using your potential, not your past. I'm not saying your past doesn't have some lessons to be learned from but it has very little ability to give an accurate definition to your personal value.

- ❒ Family, education, money, and the media are all powerful forces that desire to shape your life. The day any of those things can promise you happiness is the day you can let them take over.

- ❒ **Taking charge of our destiny sounds great, but there is one thing to consider; you can never again blame someone else. Becoming a person of destiny means giving up the right to blame. What a wonderful way to live your life.**

- The next time somebody tells you that if you don't do what he or she tells you to do they won't let you hang out with them, just smile and say I thought you were hanging around ME.

- The cares of the world choke out new ideas. $E=mc^2$ came to a young man in his twenties. Why? As we grow older our cares become what we define as responsibilities. We often sacrifice our dream life on the altar of responsibility.

- Never turn money into a moral issue. Money is the best friend of your destiny. Quit stirring up a fight between the two.

Chapter Two

7 laws of breaking the fear barrier

—*free yourself from every fear...for good!*

Once the mind is set in motion it is an unstoppable force. So make sure that you have it focused in the right direction or that force may turn against you.

Have you ever met your old friends at, for example, a high school reunion and found that they were still as immature as they were ten, twenty, even thirty years ago? They act the same, have the same interests, use the same vocabulary, laugh at the same jokes, and even wear the same style of clothes. It's as if they were frozen in time.

That is exactly what fear does to you—it freezes you in time. When you are frozen, you cannot progress, cannot grow, and cannot succeed. Whatever the fear, overcoming it requires change—***and that is precisely what causes people to lose their forward momentum.***

Those who refuse to change stop growing mentally, physically, spiritually, emotionally, and/or financially. Whatever the fear or circumstances is, the time has come to break the fear barrier! Now let me show you how.

7 laws to breaking fear

The amazing thing about fear is that if you know how to beat it in one area, you can beat it again in another area—***no matter what it is!*** When you understand the nature of fear and how to control it, there is no fear on earth that will be able to get in your way.

> Once you learn how to break through the fears in your life, it will be impossible for anyone or anything to stop you from reaching your goals.

Interestingly, any time in life that you are about to achieve something great, you hit a barrier. That barrier usually ends up being some type of fear. When you learn how to break the fear, you simultaneously learn how to break the barriers.

Here are seven laws to breaking fear in your life:

Law #1—understand what fear is

Fear has the same properties as faith. Fear looks into the future and sees negative things happening and developing as though they are facts. It exaggerates the negative and focuses a game plan based on that set of beliefs.

Faith, on the other hand, highlights the positive and a different type of life strategy is born. In religion we use faith to believe in God. We have faith in ourselves because we need to believe in ourselves. We have faith in our spouse because if we didn't have faith in our spouse we would have problems in our marriage. We have faith in our business or we wouldn't invest in it.

We have faith in many things, but what exactly is faith? Faith is when you can't see something with your eyes, but you have a sense and a confidence that it is there and that you have possession of it.

Think about the cells in your body. It hasn't been until recent history that we discovered them. Scientists had a theory about cells before they even saw them through a microscope. Many other theories about our bodies and about our cosmos existed long before the microscope and telescope ever came into existence.

That is exactly what faith is! Like a microscope and a telescope, faith is a tool that allows you to see things that other people cannot see, and fear is simply the opposite. Fear is when you CAN see something with your eyes, but you do NOT have a sense and a confidence that it is there and that you have possession of it.

When you see fear for what it is—and break it—you begin to control your future. What you see in your mind's eye will determine your future because you cannot excel and grow beyond what you can see. For example, now that we can see and understand the cell, we have been able to take incredible strides forward.

Similarly, faith is a tool that enables us to believe in things and to take incredible strides forward.

#2—know the difference between fear & respect

Fear and respect are not the same. Since none of us want our children to get hurt, we naturally tell them not to touch the stove, but should they respect the stove or be afraid of it? If they are taught to be afraid of the stove, they may grow up hungry and never learn how to cook. Obviously, being afraid of the stove is not what we want. Instead, we teach them to respect the stove, and this respect is developed through knowledge, not through fear.

Fear will keep you from your goal. If you teach children to be afraid of fire because it will burn them, then they will never learn how to harness fire because they will always stand ignorant concerning something that could actually be a benefit in their lives.

We have to understand the difference between respect and fear. Racism, for example, is full of fear and very little respect. For every person who says, "I was hurt by a black person," there are just as many people who will say they were hurt by a white person, by an Asian person, by a Hispanic person, etc. We must ask ourselves, "Is my view of another race based on fear?"

> Respect empowers you, but fear always takes power away from you.

With knowledge comes respect. That respect might cause you to stay out of certain neighborhoods and it might cause you to seek out a business relationship with someone of a different color. With fear and respect, the bottom line is this: respect empowers you, but fear always takes power away from you.

#3—set your mind in focus

As a kid I raced motorcycles. Our whole family was into it; I had one, my mom had one, my dad had one, and my brother had one. Every weekend, that's what we did.

One day as we were riding through the mountains I found myself going straight toward a cliff. My eyes were fixed on the cliff and my bike seemed to follow with absolute compliance. My dad was further up the hill and could see all this unfolding from his vantage point. He did something I'll never forget; he yelled at the top of his lungs, "Michael, look at me!"

Fortunately I was not a rebellious teen that day. My head snapped to see his voice and my bike magically followed. I was not a bad kid or a moral failure and my dad showed no anger toward me afterwards. I simply got caught in the fear zone. As soon as I changed what I was looking at, my bike changed its direction.

I never forgot that principle and realized years later that ***our lives end up going wherever we are focused.*** Focus is the key that determines our direction. Most people ignore this reality. Instead, they say things like, "You need to consider all the options" or "You need to look at this just because it's there."

Fear always tells you what to look at. Have you noticed that? Fear thinks it has the right to point out obvious things and tell you, "You don't understand." Then when you decide what you are going to do, suddenly you hear, "Have you ever thought of this? Have you ever thought about that?"

Fear always tries to seize your mind. Why? Because fear knows if you will look at fear, you will end up going in that direction. The answer is to learn how to focus on what is most important—***and fear is never most important!*** This begins by training yourself to listen to the mentors in your life.

We all have mentors. My mentor on my motorcycle was my Dad, and when he said, "Don't look over the edge," I learned to not look over the edge by focusing intently on the trail ahead of me. His voice counteracted the fear and enabled me to succeed.

Our job is to tap into those voices. If you don't have any voices in your life, then buy the CDs, audiocassettes, or videos of respected individuals who will mentor you to be fearless. Review them over and over and over so that when you are riding up the trails of life and you feel like looking over the cliff, you will hear a voice saying, "Don't look over the cliff. Keep your eyes on the trail."

This has happened to me many times. I've been able to beat the temptation to fear because of the strong mentoring voices speaking to me. It was just what I needed! I've been honored to be such a voice to others, (see reference section, pages 153-155), but whether you are speaking or listening, the goal remains the same: stay focused.

#4—keep your lights on

To "keep your lights on" means that you are someone who is always growing in knowledge, learning something new, and seeking to change. Your eyes are open and you are actively looking to better yourself. This is a good position to be in, especially when it comes to overcoming fear.

If, for example, you were in a room that you were not familiar with and suddenly the lights went out, what would you do? We would all stop because we are afraid of moving around an unfamiliar room and breaking something or getting hurt ourselves. If the lights don't come back on, we gingerly feel our way across the room and toward the door.

Similarly, if we are moving through life when suddenly our "lights" go out (we encounter a difficult situation, a barrier that appears impossible to overcome, a person who unexpectedly threatens us, etc.), we can come to a standstill. Then when no light reappears, we try our best to feel our way along.

> Out of ignorance comes fear . . . and out of fear comes nothing good.

But the truth of the matter is that you can't grow, can't achieve, and can't win in life if you are groping along in the dark! ***You are supposed to run, to soar, and*** *to move forward!* And then on top of it, most people give in to their fears if the darkness persists.

Out of ignorance has come fear.

A person's race is again a very good example of this. Ignorance has led to fear, but compounded over time, that fear has led to barriers and those barriers have prevented growth. As a result, people are missing their destiny because of fear. Never would they think, "What if part of my destiny is tied up in someone of a different race?" but it could very well be true.

> THE EDGE
> No athlete is perfect—he or she is simply better than everyone else.

Quite simply, fear has kept us from reaching our full potential. Once you recognize this fact, it is much easier to overcome the fear. The next time fear tries to influence you, realize that it is ignorance that is hurting you and seek knowledge instead. Knowledge beats fear, so turn the lights on.

#5—stay away from fear carriers

Stay away from people who are fearful and can't seem to do anything but focus on fear. Why? Because fear is contagious! It is more contagious than the most contagious disease on earth. You must quarantine it and stay away from it, and that includes the fear-ridden individuals who could potentially infect you.

What if the person happens to be someone you love? The only fearful people you should permit to be around you and your family are those you have a relationship with and you know they listen to what you say. Your spouse, your children, your family, and close friends need your help getting over their fears. However, fearful people you have no relationship with and who refuse to listen to you should not be allowed near you! Quarantine them—they are too dangerous and their fear is too contagious to deal with, so don't even try.

At the very least, allowing fear-ridden people to come in contact with you will cause you to lose your edge (your ability to do a little better than those around you). To succeed in life, you don't need to be perfect, you simply need to be better than the obstacles and opponents you face. But mixing fear into the equation will cause you to lose your edge every time.

The cost is too great. Stay away from fear carriers.

#6—listen to the right voices

You hear thousands of voices and hundreds of thousands of words in the course of one week's time. From TV to radio to the people you spend time with, there are voices everywhere. You will even hear words from your past—words spoken years ago—that still impact you.

With all the voices speaking to us, wouldn't you agree that most of the words are negative ones? Sure, we hear a few positive words now and then, but it only takes one negative word to knock out ten positive ones, and we don't usually have ten positive words on reserve. As a result, the negative words wear us down and our thinking is programmed to believe what we are hearing.

> We are programmed by what we hear.

Did you catch that? ***You are programmed by what you hear***. Once your thinking is programmed, internally you begin to believe it and then act it out.

There is one defense against the many voices battering away at you. It is your own voice through what I call "self-talk." Listening to your own voice is a powerful tool. Here is how you use it to your full benefit:

A positive word—If someone says something positive about you, then confirm that word with your own mouth. Don't be like most people who deflect the positive comment with an "it wasn't much" or "I was just lucky." To do that is to disregard the gift of a positive comment that was just given to you. It was meant to destroy fear in your life. Instead, say "thank you" and receive the words that were given to you.

Some religious people for example, will say, "It wasn't me, it's all God." If you want to say that on your own time with God, that's fine, but the compliment was given to you, not God! When people are complimenting you, thank them and receive what they are saying. It's their gift to you—and it will help destroy fear in your life.

A negative word—When a negative word comes, and you obviously can't deal with every single word, deal with the words that grab your attention and get lodged in your mind and heart. You need to challenge that word, and you challenge it with self-talk.

For example, someone came up to me not long ago and said, "I disagree with this one thing that you said." Of course it is everyone's right to agree or not agree with something I might say, but what this person disagreed about happened to be very important to me. Instead of mulling the comment over and over, I reminded myself that thousands of people's lives have been positively affected by the very point that this person was disagreeing with. "Thousands of people agree with me on this," I said to myself, "so I refuse to let this one comment get me down."

If someone insinuates that you are stupid, you need to immediately start talking to yourself, "I am not stupid! I'm intelligent. In fact, I'm smarter than that person is!"

Realize that the offending person might be ignorant, completely unable to hear and see what you are trying to say. Deal with the negative words and don't take up an offense against the individual, but never "in the name of humility" thank the person! Graciously excuse yourself and immediately tell yourself the truth: "I'm good! I'm beautiful! I'm wonderful!"

Whatever you have to say, say it, but just don't listen to the negative words.

When it comes right down to it, of all the voices that you hear, the one voice that plays the most important part in your life is your own. Use it freely to dispel fear.

#7—retrain your thinking

A friend of mine, Shake, is one of the strongest men in the world in his group and can bench-press seven hundred pounds! I've had the opportunity to be trained by Shake, but I'm a tall, skinny guy (6'4", 200 lbs.), so I'm obviously not competing with Shake. One time we were benching and I could only lift the weight three or four times. Shake said, "I'll put more weight on the next set."

I tried to argue, but he said, "We are going to do forced reps and you need more weight for that."

I was about to die with the weight as it was, so why would I want more weight! All I could imagine was a guy who can bench seven hundred pounds forcing me to lift an impossible weight. Then he explained, "Forced reps are not me forcing you; forced reps are me helping you lift more than you can lift. ***It will retrain your thinking.***"

We all know that the body can actually lift more weight than the mind will allow it to lift, which simply means that you are stronger than you think. Forced reps also force you to deal with the mental barriers that are in your life. "I can't do this!" was all I could think when Shake put an additional 270 pounds on the bar. My mind balked and my nervous system, which is there to protect me, was screaming at me to stop! But by Shake forcing me to lift the weight several times, with his help, I was able to retrain my thinking and defeat fear.

> The one voice that plays the most important part in your life is your own.

In life the same principle applies. Through forced repetitions we force our thinking to change, and when it changes, fear is defeated. So whether it's your marriage, business, family, or something else, face your fear head-on and force your thinking to change. Fear will be defeated for good.

Chapter Two

Steps to Success

❒ Fear is the opposite of faith. Faith holds a passionate view of the future. Fear is intimidated by the future and clings to the present for protection.

❒ At first glance, fear and respect look similar. But fear is accompanied by anxiety whereas respect is accompanied by confidence.

❒ **Once the mind is set in motion it is an unstoppable force. So make sure that you have it focused in the right direction or that force may turn against you.**

❒ Your focus is of great value—don't let it get ripped off. You go wherever you are focused. Treat it with the same respect as gold.

❒ Keeping your creative juices flowing will keep your mind light so that you are nimble enough to take advantage of every opportunity.

- You don't have to pick up the phone every time it rings and you don't have to listen to negative people every time they call, either.

- Remember, you can teach an old dog new tricks. Your mind will allow you to retrain it at any stage in your life.

Chapter Three

Mastering stress

—and putting it to work for you!

Maintaining your integrity will power you through stress because its nature is consistent power and the nature of stress is inconsistent confidence.

It is impossible to reach the next level without going through stress. When people talk about being stress-free, they are saying that they don't want to move to the next level. The issue is therefore not being free of stress, but managing stress, mastering stress, and even making stress work for you. Only those who have quit are living a stress-free life.

Taking a break, such as a vacation where you don't think about work and turn off your cell phone, is healthy, but overall, stress is not something you should try to run away from. People who run from stress usually end up turning to the wrong things, such as drugs, alcohol, excessive amounts of TV, procrastinating habits, etc.

We should not try to escape anything. Instead, we should try to conquer what is in our way so that we can become winners in life. That next level is a goal that we must pursue with a victorious mind-set that says, "I am not afraid of stress!"

Stress will serve you if you master it.

Learning to master stress

I was at the gym one day when a young man walked in with his friends. He was ranting and raving about his small paycheck. He pointed to the name of the individual who had signed the check and said, "I wish I had this guy's job. He makes all this money and all he does is sit around and sign checks."

The young man had no idea what stresses and responsibilities were required of the individual who signed his paycheck. To him it did look like a cushy job, but in reality the financial officer who signed the checks most likely earned every dime he made.

I would bet that if, by some twist of fate, this angry young man were to find himself in the position of signing the company's checks, he would not keep his new job for long. Why? Because he has no idea of what is required of the individual who "sits around and signs checks." Until he better understands the job of a financial officer, there is no way he could handle the stress involved.

> Get this into your thinking: Reaching the next level will require that you master stress.

For us, when we are faced with a new stress, we must overcome it; otherwise we are no better off than when we started. ***If we fail to master the new stress, we are placing a ceiling over our heads that seals our fate and our success level forever.***

I have seen people, generations of people, who refused to do just that. They were not willing to deal with stress—and they of course failed to teach their children how to handle stress. It wasn't that these people were ignorant, stupid, not good-looking enough, born on the wrong side of the tracks, etc. It is simply because they put a ceiling over their lives and refused to become good at handling stress.

To master stress, you must ***learn*** the six S.T.R.E.S.S. steps, then ***apply*** them.

Step #1: *S = strong*

In order to deal with stress, you have to be strong. Part of that strength is your ability to stay balanced. When my son, Caleb, was ten years old, he took Kung Fu. Interestingly enough, he discovered that all strength and power come from one thing: balance.

For balance to be so effective it must have integrity, which simply means that the balance is consistent. For example, if you have a piece of metal that has integrity, it has been pounded and heated, pounded and heated, etc. The stress of pounding and heating repeatedly produces integrity in the entire piece of metal. Why is that important? Because if the metal is strong all the way through, then it can handle unexpected stress evenly without breaking. ***The same principle applies to us—we must be consistently strong all the way through!***

That is what integrity is all about—being the same day in and day out. It doesn't mean that you must be perfect, but you must be consistent. I witnessed the power of this principle on my first real job as a teenager working in a bakery. My job was to clean anything and everything that was dirty. I was part of the sanitation crew, which simply meant that I was the "cleanup boy."

My dad had always taught me, "Have integrity. If you take a job, then you are there to work that job. No playing around! If you think you deserve more pay, then ask for a raise. If they don't want to give it to you, go get a different job, but if you decide to work for them, fulfill your end of the contract because they are fulfilling theirs by paying you what they said they were going to pay you."

As I minded my own business, cleaning as I was supposed to, I noticed other people wasting time. I even found one man sleeping in a locker! About that time the company went through a financial crunch and laid off most of its employees. I had no seniority and knew it was just a matter of time before they let me go as well.

Finally, they called me into the office. As the cleanup boy, I was thinking to myself, "Well, it was nice working here." The manager said to me, "We have been watching you."

Nervously I said, "Okay?"

"We have noticed something about you," she said.

I said, "What?"

"We noticed that you work, and that you work when nobody is watching." Her next words stopped me cold: "We are not going to lay you off. Instead, we are going to give you a raise."

I couldn't believe my ears! We were in the middle of the layoff and here I was getting a raise! Why? Because I was a man of integrity. Integrity helped balance my strength, enabling me to handle the stressful conditions that were around me.

When you maintain your integrity, you are proving to yourself that you can take it to the next level. You are strong.

Step #2: ***T = tension***

In trying to be more successful than you are today and reach the next level, it is important that you keep a certain amount of stress in your life. Not too much, but enough to keep tension.

Have you ever seen a tightrope act at a fair or a circus? The tightrope has just enough tension to allow the performer to walk or ride across. But with no tension the rope would droop and with too much tension the rope would snap—either way the performer falls.

Unfortunately, a lot of people fail to keep the right amount of tension in their day to day life. They have some stress but don't bother to manage it. They keep going and all of a sudden the tension goes slack or snaps and they fall. They think they need less stress, so they lower their expectations and themselves to a lesser level. Then when it happens again, they again try a lower level.

> It is important that you keep a certain amount of stress in your life.

But tension is necessary. It is important to keep a certain amount of pressure and stress on your life. It is healthy as long as you are managing it. If you can keep the tension strong and balanced, it gives you something to walk on. Without the tension you will collapse. When you understand that, it is easy to see that stress can actually serve you by enabling you to perform at a higher level.

In sports, you actually start living for stress because it makes you perform better. It also earns you more, because the person who can handle the pressure the best gets paid the most. Take Michael Jordan, for example. He was not the best shot on the court, but his ability to handle the stress of the last minute of the game put him miles ahead of the rest.

When you can handle stress, you are setting yourself up for tremendous success because you are balanced and you are able to keep going when others fall. You have just the right amount of tension.

Step #3: ***R = rest & relaxation***

If you, like me, come from a workaholic family, you have to be careful. Pushing yourself too far can cause unnecessary damage. I love communicating and speaking, but I've been on vacations before where I will get carried away and set up speaking engagements through contacts that I meet on my vacation.

I needed the rest and relaxation, but instead I stayed in the work mode. I've learned since then that I need to plan out my times of rest and relaxation. If you plan your upcoming vacation, your mind can produce at a higher level in the meantime because it knows it will get rest at a certain date in the future. If there is no rest date scheduled, it shoots fear into your life with thoughts like, "This stress may never stop."

Not having a break is not a good stress management way of thinking. When you don't have any way of knowing if there is light at the end of the tunnel, the pressure on you can cause you to be alarmed and snap under the pressure.

One pressure-filled job is that of being a mom. I salute moms for the amazing work that they do. Unfortunately, some moms, especially single moms, have to be both the father and the mother. They might work three jobs just to support the family. Work is constant, kids are constant, and there is no break in the near future. They feel trapped, and rightly so. Many completely give up because they have fear and doubt…that they will ever break out of the never-ending cycle. (If you know somebody who is a single mom, help her out.)

People who feel trapped in their situation, whatever it might be, are experiencing unhealthy stress. They need to plan for some much needed rest and relaxation. If they don't plan for a break, they will be tempted time and time again to give up and quit. When this happens, the quitter loses every time. He or she drops to the next lower level, but the stress doesn't leave! Giving up just makes it more difficult to get to the next level.

Plan for rest and relaxation...because you need it!

Step #4: ***E = energy***

In order to handle stress you must have energy. Have you noticed that when your energy level is down, stress can wipe you out? A little bit of stress and you feel sick, depressed, and you want to give up. Little things bother you. Your mind tells you that the stress level is rising—but in actuality, the stress level isn't rising, it's just that your energy level that enables you to handle the stress is lower than normal. Lack of sleep, improper eating, too much caffeine, and lack of exercise are just a few of the factors that negatively affect your energy level.

> Successful people never look like they are moving too fast. They are smooth—are you?

I had a gentleman working for me once who refused to use a day planner. I require that everyone use a day planner because I know it is a tool that helps people balance their stress, but he just wouldn't do it. After re-explaining the value of using a day planner, he told me that I was just putting pressure on him.

Later I thought about it and realized that I was indeed putting pressure on him—and that was good! A certain amount of pressure would enable him to bear the stress associated with his position. I was actually feeding him something that would energize him in the long run. He had a hard time believing it was to his benefit.

Similarly, when it comes to anything that feeds your mind, body, and soul, take it! Do what you know will feed you because it will in turn feed your energy level. Then when stress comes, you won't be knocked down. You owe it to your family, to your business, to everybody you know, and to yourself to stay full of energy.

There are times when your energy level takes priority. My wife, for example, can get so involved in what she's doing that she forgets to eat! If she denies herself for too long, it will hurt her. The same with us, whether it's physical, mental, emotional, or spiritual, if we deprive ourselves of what we need, our level of energy is going to decrease.

When you fly, the flight attendant asks you to put the oxygen mask on yourself before you help your own child. Why? Because if you pass out due to lack of oxygen, your desire to help your child won't even matter! You are not served and they are not served by helping them first.

The point is that there are times when we must take care of ourselves first. In the area of energy, if we ignore our own needs too long, the time may come when we are of no benefit to anyone. The bottom line is this: you must keep your energy level up.

Step #5: *S = smooth*

Most people don't realize that they need to be smooth. It's the little things on the outside and on the inside that make you smooth. For example, the way you carry your physical body will affect how you think on the inside. Another example is what you drink. I love coffee, but caffeine gives me the jitters and makes me nervous, so

I can only drink decaffeinated coffee. Whatever it is that ruins your ability to be smooth, drop it.

If you've noticed, successful people never look like they are moving too fast. They are always smooth. They aren't in a big hurry. You would think that successful people would be running from one important thing to the next, but they are busy and successful without losing their smooth perception. Anyone who looks frantic and hurried is sending clear signals that life is not in order, things are about to fall apart, and that you are not in control.

If "hurried and frantic" describes you, then learn how to take a deep breath and say out loud, "It's OK, I can handle it. I'm smooth." You are smooth, so stay that way each and every day.

Step #6: *S = servant*

The last and one of the most important keys to handling stress is to become a servant to other people. When you tap into other people's needs, you realize sometimes how insignificant the things you are going through really are. In a sense, you get a double blessing in your life.

First of all, it is great to serve somebody. That alone is rewarding, but you get something else out of it. You are able to walk tall and see yourself as strong enough to help others, which in turn sends signals to your mind and to your heart that are saying:

- ❐ you are strong
- ❐ you are powerful
- ❐ you are wealthy
- ❐ you are important
- ❐ you have abilities
- ❐ you have skills

All of these signals tell you that you are strong enough to handle the stress that is coming in your life. "Not only am I strong enough to handle the issues of my own life," your mind is telling you, "but I am strong enough to help somebody else."

That is a very powerful message for you to live with, and it better equips you to stand up to stress.

CHAPTER THREE

STEPS TO SUCCESS

- ❒ Running away from stress will give the blockade of stress even more power to hold you back from your dreams. So form a strategy for victory, not of retreat.

- ❒ Mastering stress should be part of your vision plan when you are reaching to the next level. Don't just bump into it on your way to the top! Plan for it.

- ❒ **Maintaining your integrity will power you through stress because its nature is consistent power and the nature of stress is inconsistent confidence.**

- ❒ Don't just rest when you are so beat up you can't stand it anymore. Make rest part of your success strategy. "Fatigue makes cowards of us all."

Chapter Four

Leaving the old behind
—*7 steps to thinking like a millionaire*

Staying open to new possibilities demands humility but the rewards are endless. Recognizing what's possible is the first step to every great success story.

The truly successful people in life understand, among other things, that you have to go out and capture your own success. They act on the belief that if you will do what you love to do, desire to do, and are inspired to do, you will always have what you want. (They also understand that if you keep on doing what you ***don't*** want to do, you cannot expect to have what you want to have.)

There is a stage before success arrives that most people miss. All they see are successful people reaching lofty dreams and they think, "Those people have it easy. It wouldn't work for me."

If you've said things like this before, recognize that ***before success comes thought***. Those who found success began by finding the right thoughts first. For example, you want to be wealthy, but ***before you will become wealthy you must think like a wealthy person.***

The problem is that most of us come from a middle-class mind-set. We try and fail, try and fail, then come up with all the reasons why it doesn't work. We get cynical, bitter, and give up. We don't know any better, much less how to think like a millionaire…*until now!*

7 steps to thinking like a millionaire

So how do millionaires think? Here are seven steps to thinking like a millionaire:

Step #1—staying open to new possibilities

Millionaires are one creative idea away from their next million. They don't dream of big things, they think of the next little thing, the next little creative idea, or the next little invention. They live for the revelation.

Yes, there are mistakes and failures along the way, but they live for the revelation. They are always thinking and looking for something new. Most of us, on the other hand, turn off our creative engines after experiencing failure, even though creativity is the key to our success.

Consider money. It is created and unlimited, but a lot of people refuse to accept that. They believe someone else has their money and that the person (or government) who has their money needs to pay up! Before we look down on people with this welfare mentality, we need to realize that this mentality is nothing more than the lack of creativity.

> As you think in your heart, so you become financially.

Are you keeping your creative engines going? Have you put your creativity "on the shelf"? People who think like millionaires do not wait for someone else to deliver their wealth—***they go out and create it.***

Our mind is created to be creative. God created us that way. I like the fact that I'm created in His image, and if that's true, then if I'm living up to my potential I will be a creator. That is where success is found.

> Millionaires understand and see clearly the greatness inside of themselves even if others haven't witnessed it.

Consider the human brain. Studies have shown that we regularly use only 10 percent of our brain's potential! But the brain uses more of its power—up to 95 percent—when it is used for prayer, meditation, dreaming, and considering a cause bigger than self.

In short, be a big thinker, be creative, and be quick to take time to dream. After all, you are one creative idea away from your next million!

Step #2—having personal illumination

Some people believe that if they think about a Ferrari or a mansion on the beach long enough they will be thinking like a millionaire. In reality, it's what you think about ***yourself*** that will produce all the things that you think millionaires think about. Did you catch that?

It is not about stuff—cars, houses, boats, and money—it's about believing you are the most valuable person on the planet. When you see the world through that light, anything is possible! The light goes on in your heart, mind, and soul. You see it and know it, and realize the rest of the world is waiting to see it.

Here are the five elements of personal illumination:

A) ***Recognize that you may not know yourself as your true self.*** Your perspective affects you internally and externally, but both might be incorrect.

Simply remain open to the fact that you might not see clearly who you are.

B) ***Do you evaluate yourself based on your past, present, or future?*** The scariest thing you'll ever face is your potential. Expectations rise with your potential, as does fear of people's expectations. Most people don't really want to live their potential because they are scared of what might be there. ***Faith is believing the future is the true you and that you deserve it.*** If you qualify yourself by your past, you will be poor. To think like a person of wealth, qualify yourself based on your potential in the future. Don't rest on what you've accomplished—there is always something more to reach for!

> Wealth is completely dependent on you to define yourself based upon your future.

C) ***The millionaire mind will pass this test*** (if you can, you are well on your way): ***write down ten great things that you've accomplished in your life.*** Was your immediate response one of anxiety or excitement? The quicker that you can define yourself based on the great things you've done, the quicker you will be able to go into your future confident in who you are and what you've done. Most of us, if we are honest with ourselves, can more quickly think of the bad things we've done. It's good to tell yourself how great you are. It becomes an attitude of an aggressive future that releases creativity into your life—all based on you and seeing you for who you are.

D) ***Your response to people when they say they don't like you or they know someone else who doesn't like you.*** In marketing, and everyone is in marketing, what others think of you is very important, but how personal do you take it? How easy is it for someone's negative comments to throw you off your vision? How you handle that pressure is vital. The millionaire mind-set says, "My vision is what's important. If people don't like me, it's based on misinformation. If they do like me, they've got the right information. I'll get the right information to them. I won't let the misinformation get to me." People's comments won't affect you if you think like a millionaire. Besides, it's not for your sake, but for their sake—their misinformation hurts them.

E) ***Having a personal vision statement.*** Having a vision statement keeps you on track and helps you take personal ownership over anything that lies ahead. When you have a purpose and you see how you can do it, you have a millionaire mind-set—an unstoppable mind-set! You have what it takes to move into your future.

Step #3—unveiling your gifts

You have every gift you will ever need inside of you. They have been there since birth. You have it all, including purpose, destiny, and vision. The challenge, however, is how you will unveil them. These four points will help:

G—Greatness. Never underestimate the value of your gift. A gift is not a gift unless it's given. No matter how small, it's still a gift. Treat all gifts with respect.

I—Integrity. Take the time to treat your gifts with integrity. Integrity means consistency. The gift you have that has consistent energy applied to it will produce a gift that will impact others.

F—Fearless. Every gift is confronted by fear. Whatever it is, fear will rise up against it. Don't mix fear with your gift. Walk fearlessly and your gift will be unveiled.

T—Timing. Your gift must be given at the right time. Gifts take time to be developed, and if it's not developed, it's not worth giving. Let your gifts be developed and then unveiled. Millionaires are the greatest givers of all.

Step #4—getting mentored

When you have a gift, you must be mentored because a mentor will pull more of your gift out of you. They will fight with you and help train you—because they want you to win.

The sooner you recognize that you are in for a battle for your life, the better. You must have a conquest mentality. You must also recognize that your mind wants to keep you where you are. Therefore, you need a trainer/mentor to take you through the path to get you where you aim to go.

> A mentor will pull more of your gifting out of you than you could do on your own.

A—How to get a mentor:

Only allow people to speak into your life who really believe you can make it to the next level. Successful people who are motivators are not automatically mentor quality. A true mentor: 1) believes you can be successful, 2) believes in you, and 3) is good at what he or she does (you can follow his or her experience).

Mentors are willing to open up their lives to you—the good, bad, and ugly. If they are not willing to do that, then they are just trying to impress you and show you how big they are. Ultimately, you will feel smaller. Leave them. Gravitate to those who see you great and who qualify as a mentor.

B—How to keep a mentor:

Many people self-sabotage their relationship with a mentor at this point, but keeping your mentor is of absolute importance. Here is how you keep your mentors:

1. ***treat them like your mom or dad*** (you respect them but know they are not perfect)
2. ***bring equity to the relationship*** (as you reach the next level, share in your rewards: credit, thanks, and financial rewards)
3. ***pursue your mentor*** (don't expect mentors to pursue you. The fact that they are willing to mentor you shows they see quality in you. Pursue them. Let them know how eager you are. If you give up on your destiny, you will no longer pursue them.)

Step #5—having dedication

You must have dedication because an idea held long enough and accurately enough will always come to pass.

That is great news! But most people quit right before they break through. The mind self-sabotages and we go back to what is normal, ***even if we don't like it!*** How can you ensure that you break through? Be extremely dedicated and have an "I will never quit" mind-set. It is dedication that will tell if your dream is a fantasy or a true vision.

Take action, get out there and try. The lessons learned will help you to keep going. It's not your successes in the beginning that matters; it's your thinking that matters. If you hang on as your thinking changes to that of a millionaire, success is right around the corner.

> An idea held long enough and accurately enough will always come to pass.

Step #6—finding and feeding your personal posture

Do you stand with confidence within? Do you demand the attention of people and have them see you for who you really are? Do you feel like you have more to give and more inside of you than what other people see?

What is especially interesting about personal posture is that other people reap the benefits of your good posture. That is why it is so important that people see you for who you really are—***and it is your responsibility to express yourself clearly.***

> Buy into the person you are on the inside.

What is common, however, is that we don't define ourselves adequately. We are sensitive because we want others to like us, but that destroys our posture. The answer is to define yourself. After all, people buy into who you are, but if they don't know who you are, how can they buy into you?

You might be wondering what posture is exactly. Some think it's self-esteem, but self-esteem is when you know who you are. Posture is self-esteem PLUS the ability to make that known to others. When you hold yourself with respect on the inside and the outside, your posture will naturally come out.

Now, how to find and feed your personal posture…

How to find your personal posture

There is a dynamic person inside of you. As you find more and more of that person, you want to take it to the next level. The more you find, the stronger you get and the more you have to give and serve people with.

To find your personal posture, there are three locators that will help:

1. ***What do people know about you?*** Do they have a sense about your purpose? If they do, then your personal posture is evident. You are letting the true you come out. If they don't have a sense about your purpose, then they are forced to define you in order to have a relationship with you—and their definition of you will not be to your liking. Of course, if you define yourself, you run the chance that they might not like you. That is still better than letting them define you.

> Posture:
> Knowing who you are (self-esteem) AND the ability to make that known to others.

Having personal posture includes the understanding that it is more important that people respect you than like you. When people respect you, your posture is evident and they can buy in to that. If they don't like you, at least you defined yourself clearly.

2. ***How do you rate yourself?*** Consider for a second what is important to you (business, family, friendships, exercise, etc.). On a scale of one to ten, with ten being "great" and one being "terrible," how would you rate yourself? Are you giving yourself perfect tens? For most of us, our tendency is to underrate ourselves.

   Whatever you rate yourself, add three more points to it. Why? Because we all rate ourselves too low—***and we live up to our own ratings!*** Be honest in a positive sense and believe more in yourself!

3. ***What do other people get from you?*** Keep your eyes open for feedback. Watch for what it is that people are getting from you repeatedly. Are they getting love, encouragement, wise counsel, friendship, advice, etc. from you? Whatever it is, notice it, for that is your key talent that people want. That is also an area where you have successfully developed your personal posture. Other people like it and even need it—and it's to their benefit.

   If people come to you, for example, for love, find out why. Examine how you carry yourself in that strength and confidence, then apply that same attitude to a different subject in your life. When you have located your posture, express that accurately and powerfully to others so that you can serve them to a greater degree.

Feeding your posture

We all market something, but do we consciously market ourselves? That is the first thing we need to market. After all, people buy you, not the product. You need to feed yourself positively by building yourself up on the inside.

A good friend of mine is one of the top marketers in the nation. The company he works with has over one hundred thousand employees in it, yet he remains one of the top producers, marketers, and trainers. I asked him how he did it and he gave me three marketing keys that, interestingly enough, are equally valuable principles for forming relationships. These principles are:

#1—*Massive action always equals massive results.* People are attracted to confidence. If there is no equity in the relationship, the relationship could be over. In marketing, when you have many leads, you don't care what others say. If others don't qualify, you don't care and you move on. In relationships, if you spend your whole life trying to keep the few friendships you have—***at the cost of your own self-esteem***—you will most likely lose some of those relationships. At the very best you will keep them, but at the cost of losing the true you to the relationship.

> In terms of success, you can't be successful if you let others define you.

#2—*Amateurs sell, professionals sort.* Not everyone cares, so let them go. Are you really serving and helping people if they are defining you? No! So define yourself and let that do the sorting for you. You are to serve other people, but you'll never serve effectively if you are trying to live up to their expectations. Acknowledging your strengths to better serve others is part of defining yourself.

When you define who you are, then you have the power and confidence to sort and not sell. If other people define you, then you have to sell yourself. In terms of success, you can't be successful if others define you.

#3—*Produce wealth in others and it will always come back to make you wealthy.* When you find a way to get what is inside of you to others to their benefit, you will prosper. Any area of prosperity through service will cause "buy in" and you will be wealthy. And how can you serve them unless they see what's inside of you—your posture. They have to see your posture and know what you have to offer.

Step #7—using your skills and becoming a mentor

Once you become successful, become a teacher and mentor for others. By doing that, you learn the principles again and again. You both win. Success isn't a mystery; it's learning the skill of successful thinking, which is nothing more than always remembering and doing the basics.

The presence or absence of gifts is not what decides if you will be successful or not. It is the use of your gifts that decides everything, for when you use your gifts they turn into skills. That is one reason why it is so important for you to mentor others.

You have much to offer because you went through the process of change to become the real you. Let your life be a powerful example to others.

Chapter Four

Steps to Success

- ❐ Success is not something that feels obligated to track you down. So if you want it you must learn how to capture it.

- ❐ **Staying open to new possibilities demands humility but the rewards are endless. Recognizing what's possible is the first step to every great success story.**

- ❐ Having a personal illumination is what life is all about. The higher you see your value the more you expect from life, and the more you expect, the more opportunities you will recognize.

- ❐ Unveiling your gifts is scary because of the potential of rejection. Most of us aren't really afraid of failure but rather the rejection that can accompany it. Just remember your critics will reject you even when you succeed so what do they know!

- ❐ Mentorship is not an option. Show me a person's mentors and I will show you their potential.

- ❐ Maintain an "I will never quit" dedication. In the summer of 1975 my dad would not let me quit a terrible job I had. He knew the job was not the greatest but simply declared to me "Son don't let that job beat you." Change, don't quit!

- ❐ Finding and feeding your posture is like finding your perfect weight and eating healthy to keep it there. Your posture is your inner appearance and strength. Get out of shape in this area and you will become weak underneath the skin.

PART II

breaking into the new

Chapter Five

Reaching the next level

—*what it takes to break into the new*

Fantasy is death to the person who truly desires success. But the problem is that fantasy and vision on the surface look and smell the same. They both have hopes and desires. What you are willing to endure will determine whether you are holding a true vision or just a fantasy.

If everyone were born with clasped hands, we would be one-handed, two-thumbed people. Life would certainly be different—tying your shoes would be a challenge, drinking from a cup would be very awkward, and shaking hands would be virtually impossible.

Now imagine you are forty years old, well accustomed to a one-handed, two-thumbed life, and one morning you wake up and your hands are suddenly separated!

Most of us would look at our hands and scream and clasp our hands back together. Though two hands and ten fingers are clearly superior, the clasped hands are what we are accustomed to—it's safe and normal.

When we broke out of the norm (from two thumbs to ten fingers), fear caused us to go back to what was safe. Our mind is like that. It demands order and, as you already know, will do everything it can to keep that order, even when it doesn't make sense.

So how do you break out? How do you fulfill your dreams? How do you get from your current level to the next level?

How to break out—7 guidelines to get you to the next level

Everyone has a different position and a different view of things. What you believe to be true and real is just a perception built upon where you are in life. That is why a millionaire sees money differently than someone who is on welfare or someone else who is a billionaire.

Have you ever been in a noisy crowd and tuned into a conversation that was taking place across the room? We all possess the ability to "tune in" and "tune out" certain sounds.

Your mind also has the ability to block out certain things. For example, you might tune out the "noise" (negative comments, criticism, anger, etc.) of a welfare-minded individual who is trying to convince you that you are wrong in your pursuit of your potential. Your success has positively affected you enough to tune out what you do not need to be hearing.

> If you are preparing for the next level of success, it will come.

But how do you know you aren't tuning out something you really ought to hear? How do you know you haven't developed blind spots that are inhibiting you from reaching the next level?

The answer is to follow the seven guidelines below—they will get you to the next level!

Guideline #1—Know the difference between fantasy and vision

Getting to the next level is not a fantasy. There is a concrete system that you can learn and practice so that you are good at moving to the next level. However, most people approach the idea of reaching the next level with "maybe some day" or "I hope I can" or "if I win the lottery."

With that mentality, you'll never make it. If you aren't paying attention to how you learn, you will never make it to the next level because ***the key to continually making it to the next level is learning how you learn.***

Everyone has been a winner in some area of life, but would you consider yourself to be a success? If you can remember the instances where you succeeded but don't see yourself as a success, ask yourself this question: "What would allow me to be a winner in one area but not a winner in another area?"

Answering that is part of the process of learning how you learn. You see, ***the problem is not in your ability to be successful—it's your ability to repeat success!*** If you could apply the same thinking and same habits that helped you be successful in one area to every other area in your life, you would be continually successful in making it to the next level. But few people take the time to understand the thinking and habits that brought them their success. Usually they stick a photo of a Ferrari or mansion on the refrigerator and wish upon a star. That is fantasy, and fantasies produce a mind-set that is unhealthy.

> The problem is not your ability to succeed.

The truth is, if you aren't doing anything to prepare for the next level of success, it will never come. It's just a hope that will some day be deferred, and you'll be mad, bitter, disillusioned, etc. That is why people who accidentally succeed or win the lottery are worse off a few months or years later. They might have more money temporarily, but they lack the internal preparation necessary to remain at that new level of success. As a result, they self-sabotage and lose it all.

Instead of fantasy, you need a vision that will produce a mind-set so strong that you can handle the ride to the top AND have the capability to stay at the top. Vision entails knowing what you want (your goal), understanding what it will take to get there, and applying yourself 100 percent to do what is required.

For example, at the age of forty I decided I wanted to play golf. I had never played and didn't know the rules, so I found a professional golfer and had him coach me (I also knew I could never figure it out on my own). I believed I could do it and practiced a lot. On my eleventh round I shot a seventy-six. I found out later that only 3 percent of golfers shoot in the seventies!

The point is that I knew what it took to succeed…and I did just that. There is nothing too complex about vision. Learning the process of succeeding will take time, but applying that process is the difference between fantasy and vision.

***Guideline* #2—Knock down the moral walls that restrict you**

People self-sabotage all the time—***and they feel morally right about it!*** How can that be? The answer is simple: they may have gotten out of a poverty situation, but their poverty mind-set hasn't gotten out of them.

And how can you be sure you don't have a self-sabotaging mind-set? The answer is in examining your pattern of thinking, which, as you know, goes like this: words produce pictures, pictures produce emotions, and emotions go on to form belief systems. Around our beliefs we naturally create moral walls to protect our beliefs.

This is all fine and dandy...***until we realize that where we want to go is not our current reality.*** People often find themselves in this predicament when it comes to money. They've developed a belief system over the years that won't allow them to reach the next level, so instead of breaking through, they accept their position as morally right...and anyone who passes them is therefore morally wrong.

That is why certain people are opposed so aggressively for making "too much" money, while others are seldom harassed. The reason for this selective opposition has nothing to do with income and everything to do with moral walls built up around people's beliefs.

Once people have built these moral walls around their beliefs, it is impossible for them individually to reach the next level. They believe they are morally right no matter how much they hate their own situation. Then, after repeated failure to get to the next level, they create false theological beliefs. I hear them all the time, such as "God doesn't want me to be wealthy" or "Whatever fate I have is what God wants for me" or "I guess it's not for me to be rich."

> You become what you expect.

Retrace your thinking back to the very words that caused you to believe what you believe—***and change those words!*** It's never too late to start over if you are willing to change.

***Guideline* #3—Reset your expectations**

Someone once said, "People don't get what they want; they get what they expect." How true! Most of us have a lot of wants, but it isn't what we want that will get us there; it's what we expect.

In sports, business, or life, those who expect to win are the ones who win. Those who expect to get to the next level will get there. That is because ***your current reality is based on your expectations.*** To break free to the next level, you need to set new expectations.

In school, do you remember what scores a "C" student would get? Most likely he got Cs. The "A" student, on the other hand, would get As. Does this prove anything? Well, if the "C" student happened to get an A, what would he say? Probably, "I can't believe it—I got an A!"

And that is precisely the problem! He doesn't see himself as anything but a "C" student. If he gets an A by accident, he'll slack off a little and settle for his C again. But if he gets a D, he'll work hard to pull his grades up so that he at least gets a C. (He doesn't want to be a "D" student, that's for sure!) He simply becomes what he expects.

How do you reset our expectations? There are two steps to the process:

A) **Step #1—challenge your beliefs about what you believe you deserve out of life.** Take the "C" student, for example. He was able to bring up his grades when he wanted to, but he wasn't willing to believe that he was capable of being an "A" or "B" student. His words "I can't believe it—an A!" defined him. To challenge your beliefs, rewrite your expectations.

B) **Step #2—keep yourself accountable to someone you can trust and who believes in you.** You need someone in your life who is trustworthy and who wants you to prosper possibly even more than you do. This person will hold you accountable to your expectations.

You owe it to yourself to break free of expectations that aren't real and to break into the next level.

Guideline #4—**Close the back door on your old level**

Reaching the next level is about closing the back door of the old level. As you move from the old level to the new level, it may feel like chaos, but that's just part of the process. If life was easy and everything was going smoothly, you wouldn't be on your way to the next level. The pressure that builds in the chaos is what helps push you up to the next level.

Chaos is what you experience when your mind, which is accustomed to order, does everything it can to stay in its current reality. But if you can press through the chaos, you will reach the next level. All the while, your mind clings to the same mental pattern that you are trying to overcome. Your mind thinks security is where you were, but that's not true.

> Chaos is not a signal saying you must go back. It is a sign that you are on the right track.

For example, if you come from the middle class, you most likely have middle-class ideals, middle-class morals, and middle-class beliefs. At the same time, faced with change, your mind will do all it can to keep you where you are comfortable, accustomed to, in control, etc. (This applies to every area of life: goals, money, relationships, etc.) The security that you feel at your old level is really a misplaced sense of security...***your mind just doesn't know it yet.***

The only way to convince your mind that the next level is where you need to be is to use order—the very thing that your mind craves—as the reason why you should get to the next level. You accomplish that by making your potential your new goal of order.

> The next level is the only security that your mind wants . . . it just doesn't know it yet.

You might, for example, believe you are worth a certain amount per year. The difference between your current pay and your believed worth is the temporary chaos that your mind must battle through to reach the next level. When your mind accepts your believed worth as real, you are well on your way!

To make sure your mind moves you forward through your temporary chaos, you must:

1. recognize that through the chaos you will have to deal with moral walls and other people's opinions—accept that fact and ignore the resistance

2. break your mind's ability to self-sabotage by closing the back door to the old and deciding that going back is not an option

When you can make breaking the chaos boundary a pattern, you can keep going through every new challenge or goal to get to the next level. Because the mind wants order so much, if you can close the back door when you get into the chaos stage, your mind will push yourself up to the next level. It will catapult you to your potential as your mind latches onto the order of the next level.

***Guideline #5*—Become other-people focused**

To get to the next level, you need people in your life. If you have to wait for others to find you and help you, it won't work. It will take forever. Instead, you need an other-person mind-set that seriously desires to help other people reach their goals. When you focus on others, you expand yourself, allowing yourself to go further than you have ever gone before.

A financial example is that of having children. People say children are expensive, and I'm not denying the costs associated with raising my three children, Michaela, Caleb, and Crawford, but did you know that on average there is a four thousand dollar per year increase in total family income per child born into a family?

> A vision for other people will force you to the next level.

"How is that possible?" you might be thinking. The answer is simple: the parent or parents became other-people focused. It ***forced*** them to the next level, and the more people you add to the capacity of your heart, the more it stretches you to the next level.

What's more, whenever you focus on others, you are closing the back door on your old level.

***Guideline #6*—Create positive discontent**

Wouldn't you agree that we all want more than we currently have? We want more money, more time with the family, more freedom, more out of life, etc. That is healthy and normal—***if you didn't want more, something would be wrong.***

Frustration comes, however, when we want more than we are willing or "able" to change to get. For example, if you want to reach a higher income level but are not willing to go through what it takes to get there, you will become frustrated. It comes down to this: change to reach the next level or keep the old order and be frustrated.

People who never come to grips with this reality often live in a fantasy world where they dream of having more but never take action to get there. There are generations upon generations of frustrated people who will never get out of their current financial situation.

Moral walls form at this point in an effort to deal with the frustration that is never released. That is why you hear middle-class people say with pride that they are the "hardworking backbone of America." They believe it's morally right to be middle class—and they have no more frustration.

Instead of accepting this dismal view, you can reach the next level by fostering discontent with your current level. When you become discontent with your current reality, the old is no longer comfortable and you can sell yourself on moving to the next level. Your mind buys into your new reality and helps propel you toward your vision.

For example, if you start looking at a new car, what usually happens? You buy one, right? You do so because after sitting in the new car, touching and smelling your "new reality," you:

- realize your new reality is real,
- realize your new reality is achievable, and
- realize you are discontent with your old reality.

As a result, returning to the old reality (old car) is no longer an option. You have successfully sold your mind on your new reality, thus keeping you from self-sabotaging as you move forward.

Guideline **#7—Learn to live in your vision reality**

A tangible car is one thing, but how do you sell your mind on an intangible new reality? It's not really that difficult. As I've mentioned, I started golf at age forty and shot a seventy-six on my eleventh round. But something happened after my tenth round that set me up for success.

I was driving my twelve-year-old son Caleb home when he asked, "Dad, are you going to join the PGA tour?"

"Of course not," I said. "I'm forty, a new golfer—there is no way!"

He said in a matter-of-fact way, "I think you could do it." Then he added, "I'm going to be on the PGA tour."

I responded to his dream as a typical father would with, "That's great! I believe you can do it!"

Then I started to think: "I believe in Caleb, but I don't believe in me. Why is that?" My logical and rational current reality, which is absolutely necessary for responsible people, told me the facts:

> When you can't self-sabotage, your mind will find a subconscious way to catapult you to the next level.

- I'm too old
- I'm too inexperienced
- only 125 professionals make it to the PGA Tour
- the chances of me making it to the PGA Tour are zero

My son, as is expected at that age, was living in his vision reality. He believed that he could do anything in life. We all had the same vision reality when we were young, but as we mature our vision reality is exchanged for a current reality. Pressures of work, life, money, retirement, saving, home, family, etc. cause our current reality to expand and our vision reality to shrink.

Caleb was the opposite. He was still living in his vision reality and I knew that by being rational and logical with him (as I was with myself), I would undermine his vision and belief in self. But why should I put down my own dream and promote his?

I realized that I didn't want to be on the PGA Tour, but why not allow myself to have a vision reality? The next day I acted like a twelve-year-old and I envisioned myself hitting the ball onto the green from hundreds of yards away. I started speaking to my subconscious mind that I could do it, that I could be Tiger Woods, that I could make it on the PGA Tour, and more. I saw things beyond my current reality as I teed up for my eleventh round.

Within fifteen hours of speaking with my son, I went from a mid-nineties score to shooting a seventy-six! The professional golfer who had given me only two lessons looked at me and said, "Can you help me with my thinking?" (Since then I've continued to shoot in the seventies and low eighties.)

Using visualization and affirmation—allowing yourself to dream, allowing a different image of self into your life—will affect you in every area of life, from your family to your finances and from your business to your belief in self.

Anything less than your vision reality is beneath you…and you move to the next level.

Chapter Five

Steps to Success

- **Fantasy is death to the person who truly desires success. But the problem is that fantasy and vision on the surface look and smell the same. They both have hopes and desires. What you are willing to endure will determine whether you are holding a true vision or just a fantasy.**

- Many times we build up false moral beliefs about success and wealth. Morality is a gift that should serve us. It should not become our excuse for staying in our comfort zone. Good morality should challenge us to be great and not settle for mediocrity.

- Remember, seldom if ever, do we get what we want. Expectations are when we take our wants and desires and combine them with commitment and self-esteem.

- Closing the back door on your old way of thinking causes your mind to change and think only in the direction you have given it. UP, UP, UP!

- Become an other-focused leader. The drive to serve others is not just a good thing to do. It develops a positive moral obligation to prosper and win in life. As a dad I can't afford to shut down or self-sabotage. As you add other people's needs to your vision, you secure your ambition to reach higher. This one really works!

- ❐ Learning to live in what I call your "vision reality" is simply a technique where you carry out the disciplines of your new life before you actually get there. In other words, if you desire to be successful, you might want to keep a day timer before you really even need one.

Chapter Six

Prosperity consciousness
—*how to think at the next level*

Without developing a moral obligation to prosper most people will default back to their norm and justify their fear of the next level by creating a moral argument against it.

You have a moral obligation to prosper.

Several years ago I was having lunch with a businessman in a restaurant when I casually mentioned how valuable we are as individuals because of the value that God puts on us. He didn't understand what I meant, so I explained, "A painting is only worth what someone is willing to pay for it, right? Once paid for, the value is established forever."

He agreed.

I then said, "God gave His only Son for you and for me. God could have easily paid a huge sum of money for us, but he chose to give what was most valuable: His Son, Jesus Christ. Being the wise businessman that He is, I don't think He would pay more than something is worth, correct?"

My friend smiled and agreed.

At about that time a lady from a nearby table walked over and interrupted. Very agitated and clearly upset, she pointed her finger at my friend and said, "You are NOT worth that much to God!"

I was shocked at her statement and told her I disagreed entirely. Before she stormed out of the restaurant, she went on to tell me about how worthless and valueless we are as human beings. I could tell by looking at her that she didn't believe she was worth it. It was in her demeanor, in her attitude, in her frown, in what she wore, in how she walked, etc.

> Release into your destiny the great dreams that were put there by God.

I'm sure it was also reflected in her finances. She didn't believe she was worth God's Son (if we aren't worth it, why would He have paid the price that He did?), which shows me that she had a moral problem with placing value on herself. With that being the case, her pattern of thinking most likely disqualified her from ever achieving wealth.

Don't ever let such a limiting view affect you like that!

You have a moral obligation to prosper

You need to make it your moral obligation to prosper. If you do, then when things aren't going so well, you will be uncomfortable, discontent, and passionate about pressing forward until you reach the next level. It's all part of having a prosperity consciousness.

To begin with, there are two levels of prosperity that everyone deals with:

1. prosperity on the inside (how you see yourself)
2. prosperity on the outside (the circumstances, people, situations, problems, etc. around you)

What you want to do is learn how to walk in prosperity from the inside out, rather than from the outside in. Most people allow the outside, the negative thinkers and daily situations around them, to affect how they view themselves. The next-level thinker, on the other hand, ***takes what is on the inside and then demands that everything on the outside submits or comes in line with that vision***.

What this means is that there is no status quo. There is always another level to aspire to, because no matter what level you reach, if you stay there too long, you will grow bored with it. That is why maintaining a next level, prosperity-conscious mind-set is so important.

Getting to that next level, however, is no walk in the park. There will be barriers that you will need to overcome along the way, including these:

3 barriers to prosperity consciousness

We all have what it takes to prosper beyond where we are presently. We have the tools, the abilities, and the gifts to make it to the next level, but surprisingly, most of us reject prosperity when it comes. We reject the next level and many times don't even see it when it comes into our lives.

The key is learning how to receive and be ready for prosperity when it comes…regardless of any barriers.

Barrier # 1: Pressure from increase

Prosperity brings pressure because it brings increased responsibility. This causes some people to panic, but responsibility is simply "responding with ability." What this means is that the more responsibility you have, the more ability you have to respond to the things around you.

Did you catch that? You have more ability when you have more responsibility. This is obviously a good thing, but we have been programmed to see pressure as a bad thing. This type of pressure will benefit you because it will push you to the next level…if you will allow it to.

For example, if you see a family in need and you have more than they do, you are "response-able" to help. You have to determine what you will do, what you will say, what type of impact you will have on the family, etc.

> The more prosperity you have, the more "response-ability" you have.

Subconsciously most people don't want that extra pressure. "It is hard enough to keep our own lives together," they reason, and try to pass off the pressure. In so doing, they self-sabotage—***then they complain about not getting the opportunities that others are getting to expand, increase, and move to the next level!***

Those who are "response-able" have pressure…and prosperity.

***Barrier* #2—The reality of change**

We are creatures of habit who love what is comfortable. We sit in the same place, go to the same restaurant, eat the same foods, etc. If we change our routine, the change is more than most people can handle.

For example, I used to be forty pounds overweight. As I exercised, ate better, and thought differently about myself, other things began to change around me as well. I even found that some people were jealous and treated me differently! I certainly didn't expect that, but I learned that prosperity consciousness and next-level thinking will always cause change—and other people are uncomfortable with it!

When you take our life to the next level or even have just one victory, people will say, "You've changed.

You aren't the same person." Instead of being ashamed, take it as a compliment and say, "Thank you!"

Change is good and necessary, ***for if you don't change, you won't keep the prosperity that does come to you.***

***Barrier #3*—Wealth exposes weaknesses**

We hear all the time of professional athletes who are neither accustomed nor prepared to make millions of dollars a year that self-destruct in crashed cars, broken marriages, drugs, etc. But whatever the situation or vocation, it's really all the same: wealth exposes weaknesses.

If you take several kids from the ghetto and put them in a beautiful hotel, they will get edgy, paranoid, and wonder what they are doing there. It's only natural because how they see themselves does not match their surroundings. I was in a five-star hotel in the Bahamas several years ago that was absolutely incredible! I was relaxed and enjoyed my time there because how I saw myself was in harmony with my surroundings.

The goal of prosperity consciousness and next-level thinking people is to have harmony on the inside with what is on the outside. When that happens, wealth can no longer expose your weaknesses because you have accepted change and dealt with those weaknesses.

From barrier to breakthrough—5 laws of prosperity consciousness

Next-level thinkers have a concrete mind-set that is grounded on the laws of prosperity consciousness. The laws work consistently, enabling prosperity-conscious individuals to always reach the next level. Here are five of those laws:

***Law #1*—The law of attraction**

Do you know people who are insecure? They attract like-minded people to themselves, while confident people attract other confident people. The same principle applies to your wealth—***for how you think about wealth will determine your future financial success.***

It's simply a matter of attraction. What you see on the inside, your subconscious mind will try to find a way to make a reality on the outside. That is the law of attraction. And since attraction comes in degrees, it only makes sense to maximize your attraction!

What you see is what you get.

To expand your ability to attract wealth, you must first increase your vision. If you ask the average person if he or she would like a million dollars, the answer would be a resounding "Yes!" But if you asked what the million dollars would be used for, you would hear, "Um, a boat, maybe a car and a house. Other things like that."

I understand that a million dollars will buy lots of "things," but it's easy to tell that person has never thought it through—***for if there is no plan to use it, there is no plan to make it***. In addition, if there is no plan to make it, there is no plan to keep it.

What you need is a reason or vision for having wealth. When you have a vision, you will continue to attract wealth because your subconscious mind does not stop, your creativity does not stop, and your plans do not stop. However, if you don't have an active vision, the moment wealth comes into your life, you are already preparing to self-sabotage.

Did you catch that? When wealth comes to you, if you don't already have a purpose planned for it, you have already set yourself up for self-sabotage. The answer is to get a vision and purpose for the wealth you are attracting BEFORE you attract it.

***Law* #2—The law of inheritance**

All wealth is inherited. You may not inherit it from your parents, but your ability to get to the next level will be inherited through mentoring relationships, nonetheless.

Have you ever heard, "The meek shall inherit the earth"? This has nothing to do with being lowly and mild, and everything to do with placing yourself under a mentor to accomplish a specific goal. This only makes sense, since a mentor will be at the level (or higher) that you are aspiring to.

> Leadership is the ultimate in prosperity consciousness.

I know a young man who has more than a dozen mentors. Jokingly, he says he "collects mentors," but this young man is already making hundreds of thousands of dollars a year. It will be millions of dollars a year soon, simply because all of his mentors are millionaires.

Ask people you want to be like if they will mentor you. Most likely they will agree. Then do exactly what they say to do because the mind-set you are borrowing will get you to the next level.

***Law* #3—The law of the servant-leader**

Those who make it to the next level are servants. You must become a leader as well, despite the negative examples of leadership that abound. I'm sure you've experienced the leader who wants to stay ahead of you and put you down whenever you succeed (the Invalidator-Leader) and the leader who tries to control you through fear and intimidation (the Controlling-

Leader). These leadership styles are shortsighted and temporary at best.

To reach the next level, become a Servant-Leader because:

1) Servant-Leaders have the strongest foundation. When you servant-lead or mentor, it lays a stronger foundation in your own life. I used to teach tennis, and even if I was teaching absolute beginners, the next day I would have a better stroke because I was teaching the fundamentals.

As we grow and succeed, we tend to forget the fundamentals that brought us there. But if you are constantly mentoring and serving other people, it reminds you of the fundamentals.

2) Servant-Leaders benefit from any goal accomplished. Accomplishing a goal is powerful, and it's just as powerful when the goal is that of the person you've mentored. You experience the reward as well. I am positive and always optimistic because I have numerous testimonies running through my head of people I have served and helped achieve important goals. In a sense, they were my goals because I helped bring them to pass—and that is a powerful and constant reminder!

3) Servant-Leaders multiply themselves. If you have the mind-set of a servant/leader, you are not trying to invalidate people or put them down. You are not using fear and intimidation. Instead, you want them to have everything you have, which means you are developing powerful people around you who might some day surpass you. In addition, because you have multiplied yourself, you have placed yourself in the position to synergize with the very people you have mentored.

Together you can accomplish ten times what you could by yourself! That is truly awesome in its potential and will explode your prosperity consciousness to the next level.

***Law #4*—The law of language**

Whatever comes out of your mouth goes back into your ears; whatever goes into your ears gets down into your heart; and whatever is in your heart will come back out of your mouth. This can be good if the words are positive, but terribly damaging if the words are negative. (Further reason why not to listen to the words of those who are trying to define you according to their standards.)

Have you heard the proverb that says, "faith comes by hearing"? It's true. Whatever you hear the most is what you will believe and have faith in. Why not take some of that control and use it yourself to control how you think about who you are so you can have that powerful, positive, optimistic outlook on your future?

> Use affirmations to give yourself a moral obligation to succeed.

Here are two important truths to help you do just that:

#1) The power of affirmations. Affirmations train your subconscious to see yourself in a certain way. Remember, whatever you see is what you will become. The subconscious is like a sponge and receives things as though they are fact.

For example, when you say, "I am a millionaire," your subconscious doesn't argue with you, though your conscious mind might. Your subconscious absorbs and takes in like a sponge all the information, whether negative or positive, and receives it as fact. Then it begins to build on those facts and create a mental image on the inside of you based upon what you tell it!

Because of this, affirm your subconscious. Sell it on what you are now, not on what you want to become some day in the future. For example, "I *am* a millionaire" is an affirmation, while "*Some day* I will be a millionaire" will do nothing for you. It is important to know the difference.

If you allow your affirmations to be absorbed into your subconscious, your subconscious will open up opportunities in your mind that will create opportunities around you—***because it wants to make sure the outside reality matches up with its inside reality!***

#2) The power of self-talk. Self-talk is not an affirmation; it is you talking positively to yourself and taking control of a situation at the very moment that something negative occurs. This is vital because your success has more to do with how you handle negative input than it has to do with having positive input.

> Bypass your consciousness when it comes to next-level thinking.

Have you ever noticed how the home team has more energy than the visiting team? It's the self-talk coming from the crowd that makes the difference. If the home team does anything right, the crowd goes crazy.

Get a little crazy for yourself and use self-talk to keep you motivated. Remember, your success isn't always based just upon how positive you can be but how well you handle negative things when they come at you.

Here is some positive self-talk:

- I am going to make it!
- I am a winner!
- You can't beat me twice in a row!
- I will not be denied!

The law of language is something you must practice for prosperity consciousness and next-level thinking.

***Law # 5*—The law of sovereignty**

It is impossible to go to the next level if you are not a sovereign, free individual. To be sovereign does not mean to be free from laws. Instead, it means to self-govern. That is why defining yourself rather than allowing someone else to define you is so important.

To self-govern means that you take back the control that others have of your life. If you don't become sovereign, people will not be able to trust you completely because other people are still the ones making decisions for you.

High-performers, next-level thinkers, and prosperity-conscious people will not give up their personal sovereignty. They understand that maintaining their sovereignty is a requirement for success.

Be sovereign, be self-governed, and you will make it to the next level.

Chapter Six

Steps to Success

- ❐ **Without developing a moral obligation to prosper most people will default back to their norm and justify their fear of the next level by creating a moral argument against it.**

- ❐ We must prepare for the pressure of increase. Think about it this way:success weighs something. Success is not a blessing but rather provides you the opportunity to become one.

- ❐ Wealth doesn't create a weakness; it only exposes who you are. If weakness is not looked at honestly we destroy any opportunity for sustained success. Wealth gives you feedback on your maturity level.

- ❐ Prosperity consciousness is your level of assumed success—what level you demand from life. If you truly believe you deserve more, your mind goes to work 24/7 to maintain that level. Your sanity is at stake and your mind treats the threat of losing its order very seriously. I couldn't maintain sanity at a thousand dollars a month but if you can, you will probably stay there.

Chapter Seven

Rewriting your history books
—*ensuring that you never go back*

Setting high expectations is a way of reprogramming your mind. When you expect more it opens your mind to see opportunities that might have been sitting in front of you all along.

When two countries go to war, usually the victor takes the wealth of the losing nation (*to pay for expenses*) and removes or destroys the religious artifacts and artwork (*to influence the culture*). The victor takes one additional step that has more of a long-term impact than the first two by far: ***the victor rewrites the history books*** (*to control the facts that the people are led to believe*).

As time goes by, the rewritten history is believed—and the future reflects it.

The same occurs on an individual basis. Your history, whether you wrote it or someone else did, defines your future. What you can do, what you become, and what you believe about yourself are a direct result of your history.

But what if your history was written incorrectly?

Writing your *own* history

You must write your own history. If you have already come to believe you can't do or be certain things, ask yourself where the disqualification came from, who said you couldn't do it, why you believed it, etc. Then confront that lie and break it.

Believe that you have the right and the ability to do whatever it is that you aim to do. People will live ***DOWN*** to their own expectations, based on their history, but you can live ***UP*** to your expectations.

Did you know that more than 75 percent of the millionaires in the USA don't have a college degree? Whatever your situation, who cares what anyone says! Who cares what your history books say! Define for yourself who you are and what your history will be.

As you define yourself, be very careful whom you allow to give you input. Listen only to those who believe in you, who believe with you, who believe you can have more, and who know you can do it. It can be a spouse, mom, dad, son, daughter, best friend, etc. It isn't how close they are or if you work with them, but rather do they want you to succeed as much or more than you do?

> What you believe about your past will define what you believe you can receive in your future.

If you allow those who you are intimidated by or those who are perpetually negative to give you input, the results will always be the same: they will write your history incorrectly. Never hand them your history books!

To the trusted few, say, "My aim is to reach this goal, but I feel I'm not qualified. Why is it that you believe so much in me? What is it you see in me? What is it you see in my history? I need to know because it will help me combat my own self-sabotaging comments."

Their answer will help you define yourself as more powerful than you could have defined yourself. You need to use this ammunition to help you get where you need to go.

Expect resistance

When you write your history, expect resistance from invalidators (those who seek to lead you, minimize you, manipulate you, and keep you at the old level). Don't see them as your enemy—*just ignore them!*

> Invalidators seek to lead you, minimize you, manipulate you, and keep you at the old level. Just say NO!

You don't need any more people to take your value away from you. You are a powerful person who is going to the next level, and that means you simply have no time for the invalidators of life.

But the fact is every vision will have invalidators attached to it. Your challenge is to learn to spot the invalidators before they have a chance to tear you down. Typically, invalidators:

1. **are not necessarily smarter than you.** They simply want to tear down your intellectual strength.
2. **have a hard time going inward and examining themselves**. A healthy person knows that self-examination is part of growth.
3. **want you to self-examine**. They know that you are healthy and that you will at least give their negative comments some thought. The moment you go

inward to self-examine, you are weak and able to be controlled. It's natural, and they control you every time.

4. **could be anyone you know**: family, stranger, boss, etc. Whoever it is, don't listen.

How to stop invalidators

Part of writing your own history includes taking responsibility over your own mind and heart and subconscious. Invalidators, on the other hand, don't want you to take control—they want to control you.

Here is how you stop invalidators from messing up your history books:

Stopping the invalidators #1 —"No thank you!"

If the invalidators you face happen to be family members, then say, "I don't receive what you are saying. I don't want you to continue doing this. Please respect me and let me think about this later."

Then walk away and don't think about it later. They think you will go inward and self-examine, which is where they gain power over you, but it is important that you don't self-examine, ***especially not right there in front of them!***

By deleting their words from your memory, you are protecting yourself and taking away their power to write your history.

Stopping the invalidators #2 —Fight fire with fire

Don't underestimate the power of words, because words eventually become beliefs and moral walls. Negative words spoken over you can reshape your emotional base, so fight those words with your own words. After the barrage of negative words, hit yourself with a barrage of positive words. Even tell yourself, right there in front of your invalidator, what you believe about yourself.

The negative words will come back later, so be prepared to flood your mind with more positive words. When you are tempted to self-examine, don't! Speak those positive words over you again and again. Repeat what you believe about yourself until those negative words are gone.

***Stopping the invalidators #3* —Defense is unnecessary**

If you are successfully withstanding the comments of your invalidators, they will start asking you questions so they can trap you in never-ending conversations. By nature (because you are a healthy individual) you feel the need to respond and tell them why you think what you think, ***but you don't need to defend yourself!***

Now is not the time to discuss your beliefs, much less self-examine! Self-examine only with the people you can trust completely because they are the only ones who believe in you completely. I only self-examine in prayer (with God), with my wife, and with a few close confidants because they are the few who believe 110 percent in me. Simply put, keep invalidators out of your life.

Start with your past

When I was fourteen years of age, my parents divorced. Suddenly my relationship with my father was gone. He felt guilty about it, didn't know how to remedy the situation, and as a result, made me feel guilty for not calling him enough, as if I was the one not keeping the relationship alive.

As an adult, I now understand that he felt guilty and that he placed some of his pain on my fourteen-year-old shoulders, but it still affected my history. The word "relationship" conjures up thoughts of blame, pain, and pressure for anything that might possibly go wrong.

> You must recognize your value first before your subconscious will allow you to attempt to reach your new dream.

Instead of living in that condition, I've gone back to that moment in my past and rewritten my history book. I've already talked to my children and told them, "I will always call you, so you don't have to worry about our relationship. I take the responsibility to always pursue you."

By taking responsibility for my past, I am putting my spin on my history. The same principle applies to your financial, emotional, spiritual, and mental success. Whatever the past, it can be rewritten—put any spin you want on your history. The sky is the limit. Who cares if nobody else in your family has done what you want to do! Go for it! It's not anyone's business but your own what you decide to accomplish in your life.

When you realize that you have the right to write your own history books, it will bring into the present what had been held captive in the past.

Continue with your present

Most people live in the present, responding to the elements that are affecting their lives. A bill comes in the mail and they struggle to pay it, the IRS calls and they panic, a relationship goes sour and they spiral into depression, etc. Their entire life is based upon responding to what is going on around them.

> You have the right to rewrite your own history books.

As a next-level thinker, however, you don't respond to things. Instead, you demand that things respond to you. You expect things to happen; you don't wait around. You are the one who initiates change because you are in charge. You don't allow outside visions to control your inward vision. Any time you have a fear or you have an anxiety based upon outside circumstances, take a moment to see it a different way. Close your eyes and visualize that thing completely different from the inside out.

For example, not long ago I had a dark spot that started to grow on my tongue. It was pretty nerve-wracking because I make my living as a communicator. On top of it, my mom died of cancer of the mouth. My wife looked at the growth and said, "I really don't mean to alarm you, but you should probably go get it checked out."

All types of fears, thoughts, and "what if..." scenarios were running through my mind. I closed my eyes and I visualized and saw my tongue completely healthy and normal. I didn't see the growth evaporating; I didn't even acknowledge it was there. I just saw my tongue perfect and healthy and clean. I said, "God, I believe it is gone." I was choosing not to allow outside things to define who I am.

I went and looked in the mirror directly after that—and my tongue was completely perfect! What happened? I did not allow outside things to define my current reality and my present.

Regardless of your situation, you cannot allow anything to control your present. On occasion, use your visualization to see yourself from the inside out. That's how you live from the inside out to rewrite your present.

Finish with your future

All of us have more potential than we have activated in our lives. If you close your eyes and you allow yourself to dream, you will dream huge dreams, but why then do most of us settle for a life so far below our potential that you couldn't even know we had larger dreams? The answer, I believe, is our history—and it will continue to affect us.

The rewriting of your history is of course a process, but to make sure you tap into your potential, there are three important steps to take:

> **Step #1—surround yourself with those who believe in your potential.** And don't hang out with anyone who doesn't believe you have a future! Get rid of them.
>
> That might sound harsh, but those who truly love you should believe you have great potential. If they don't believe you have potential, then they are in error, they are actually out to hurt you, and eventually they will be somebody who destroys your life. Get rid of them!
>
> If they are family members who dare to talk against your potential, either ignore them or ask them, "Are you saying that I should not have this and

should not accomplish this? Is that what you are saying?" Most of them will back down if you just confront them with their minimizing attitude. Many times they don't even realize what they are saying (because they are naturally negative).

Step #2—create a vision statement. You need a big picture idea that controls your life. I always tell people my vision statement (my purpose) for what I do, which is to develop powerful people to win and influence their city, nation and world. That's it! My statement keeps my vision in focus. I also have it hanging on the wall in my office as a constant reminder.

Our family adopted the same vision statement. That means my children are getting a vision already to be developers of people. When they play soccer, they need to think about what it might be to be the captain of the team because that's part of a development process. If they are going to be around little kids, that means that they are not going to be able to bully those kids because they are there to develop little kids.

> **SUBCONSCIOUS REALITY**
>
> Write down ten things that you would like to grow in or achieve. Beside each one, write down why you think you are qualified to do it. If you do, your subconscious will tell you that you are qualified. Then live up to your expectations.

They have a mind-set or picture that is bigger than their present needs and it challenges them and everyone else to constantly push forward for a higher potential.

Step #3—set goals. When it comes to your future, set goals rather than dream of winning the lottery. The lottery isn't evil, but it does take up valuable time. Living in a fantasy is of no value to you or your family. It trains your mind to think of your future in terms of luck and fate rather than responsibility and discipline.

Instead, take control of your destiny. Set realistic short-term goals. Give yourself little victories. Write them down. ***You are rewriting your history by doing so!***

Then set mid-term goals, such as a home, a vacation home, another car, where you will go on a certain wedding anniversary, etc.

Then set long-term goals. Consider your legacy; what do you want to leave behind? What do you want people to be saying about you a hundred years after you are gone?

It's ***your*** history you are writing. You are, after all, the victor, so you can write absolutely anything you want!

CHAPTER SEVEN

STEPS TO SUCCESS

- ❒ Take ownership over your own history. Remember you and you alone have the right to interpret its meaning. Turn your history into your advantage and put your own perspective on everything. "Nobody has the right to make you feel average without your permission."

- ❒ Remember that resistance is always going to come. I had one person tell me that that was a negative belief of mine. I responded by asking them why they would resist me like that. (lol.)

- ❒ **Setting high expectations is a way of reprogramming your mind. When you expect more it opens your mind to see opportunities that might have been sitting in front of you all along.**

- ❒ I only open up my success vision fully to people who believe in my potential. There are some people close to me that I don't open up with. There are others not so close but they see my potential. I love my children but their immaturity only allows me to share so much. You need potential partners; keep your eyes open for them—they are worth more than gold!

- ❑ Every person should have a vision statement. It should state "my vision is" or "my purpose is to________________."

- ❑ Many people have a hard time setting goals because they have not first established their vision and purpose statement. When you set your vision in motion, your goals will flow through your mind. They will go right through your hand onto the paper faster than you can write.

Chapter Eight

Staying in the zone

—*6 principles to permanent progress*

Reminding yourself and holding yourself accountable to being a person of destiny is key to your self-esteem. Remember in order to estimate the true value of your life vision you must keep the blueprint bright in your mind.

All great athletes stay in the zone. They maintain the attitudes and skills necessary to stay in that high-energy, high-efficiency position. They are continually growing and moving forward and it pays off in incredible ways.

The truth is, the highest paid athletes stay in the zone the longest. Consider that! And you can live in the zone in business, family, relationships, etc. It's an attitude that effectively closes the back door to the old level and pushes you to the next level.

Here are six principles to staying in the zone:

#1—develop a selfless purpose

If your purpose is to help others, your vision and wealth will increase. It's that simple. So if you want to expand, learn how to serve others and include them in your vision. It isn't about you or a vision statement that is self-centered, such as "*my* purpose is to develop *myself* to become a powerful person to influence *my* city, *my* nation, and *my* world." If all I do is focus on my vision, my vision cannot get any larger.

To get into and stay in the zone, develop a selfless purpose—and rest assured that provision always follows vision.

#2—build your self-esteem (estimated value)

Why do people have low self-esteem/estimated value? Because people are selfish and have self-centered vision. When your vision is big, as you know, it expands your ability and pushes you to the next level. You will be fulfilled and enabled to break out of the comfort zone.

As that occurs, you will find that you are not only staying in the zone, but your self-esteem is growing by leaps and bounds. Here are three specific actions you can take to increase your self-esteem:

1. **Defeat the invalidator!** There are enemies to your personal value. Protect your values; don't let anyone invalidate you. Our need to be loved causes many to trade in their own value of self. You'll lose if you allow anyone to invalidate you—don't trade it for anything!

2. **Remind yourself constantly that you are a person with a destiny and a purpose.** You were created to accomplish something that will affect the world. Believe that you have something important to offer, expect it to come to pass, and then live up to your sense of purpose and destiny!

3. **Surround yourself with people of destiny who are going places.** Look for people who are going places. They are people of destiny. Join with them because that relationship will build your value and build your esteem.

#3—recognize your potential

Staying in the zone is obviously the place to be, but some people won't accomplish their vision simply because they don't believe they are worthy of it. Such a belief zaps your power and knocks you out of the zone, much like a needle lets the air out of a balloon.

The way to stay in the zone is to recognize your true potential. Close your eyes (just like in Chapter One) and imagine that tomorrow you wake up and every gift, talent, idea, and ability you have, including the ones you don't have time for, come out at once. You are operating at 100 percent peak performance, twenty-four hours a day, for one full year!

> The person who understands your potential the most reaps the most benefit from your life.

Repeating what I said in Chapter One, how much would that be worth? Be conservative. How much wealth would that produce? The average person says between five to twenty million a year. The number reflects your true estimated value. The gifts are yours, not someone else's gifts. That is your potential—and it's VERY valuable.

Now, consider this: If a bank loans you one hundred thousand dollars at 10 percent interest, over thirty years they will collect three hundred thousand dollars off of your loan of one hundred thousand dollars. They can do that because they are loaning you the money and because they understand your earning potential. They know what you are worth to them over thirty years, so they are more than willing to loan you the money.

The principle is obvious: ***The person who understands your potential the most reaps the most benefit from your life***. Conversely, if you don't understand your own potential, someone else will benefit more from you than you will from yourself.

Take your potential and give it courage to stay in the zone!

#4—create unstoppable desire

Desire is built upon the foundation of your potential. If you drop one thousand dollars on the ground, people will dive on it. Their energy jumps instantly up and they move with unstoppable desire. They'll even get into a fight because they see the value of it.

But, take the same one thousand dollars and tape it to the top of a skyscraper and our desire drops to almost nothing. The value of the money is the same, but we see our own potential as less than capable. This temporary desire that evaporates quickly is exactly what hype is. It won't keep you in the zone. It is a quick emotion that leaves you as quick as it comes, but something that drives you, charges you to go after your potential, is true desire.

Here is how you build true, unstoppable desire:

1. **Don't feel guilty about wanting things in life**. Passion and desire are within us. It is not wrong to desire more, to want more. If you want more but don't believe you should have more, you will self-sabotage and not get more. Break out of your comfort zone. Desire more. If what you desire is out of

good vision, good self-esteem level, good potential level, etc., then it's good for you.

2. **Develop conviction**. You must have conviction in what you are doing. When pressure comes without a solid base of conviction, things will collapse. You need to be convicted about your desire completely. Is your desire level strong enough to keep you in the game despite the pressure and chaos? The ones who make it through and appear to be untouchable are the most convinced and committed, which is based on the understanding of their potential.

> Winners are the most committed, and commitment is based on understanding your potential.

#5—remain focused

You will only be as successful as you are focused. If you stay on track, success will come. It's inevitable!

To develop focus that drives you to your destiny, you must:

1. **Keep your eyes on the road.** Don't look at the negatives around you. Don't waste your time. Your focused purpose should screen out the negatives, and besides, who cares what others think or say? Looking at the negatives will cause you to lose focus.

   Looking at every option is not being responsible, regardless of what people say about "considering all the options." Looking at the right thing is responsible. Develop the discipline not to listen to certain people, read certain books, etc. Stay committed and move forward toward your vision. Getting off focus can hurt the success of others through you.

2. **See focus as faith.** Live from within, not externally. See things in your future as more real than the situations around you. Line your focus up with your vision. It will keep you excited, bright, and vibrant. After all, who is to say that the situations around you are more real than what you are focused on?

#6—be successful

Something in you has always desired to have more and make it to the next level. When you stretch to the next level, people or things will try to pull you back to the old comfort zone. To stay in the zone where progress is permanent, you must know what success is all about.

> Success is when you begin to have more.

Success is when you begin to have more. Whatever it is, money, love, time, or freedom, when you have more, you are successful. And as you become more and more successful, you will need to learn how to live with more. You will be perceived differently, you will have more responsibility, and you will change.

Unfortunately, the pressure and issues that come from having more (being successful) are greater than some people can handle. They self-sabotage and lose it all. This should not be!

Here are four principles that will help you maintain your success:

1. **Grow in your management skills.** When your success begins to increase, your management skills will be based on the level you were at, not where you are in the midst of your increase. To avoid being outpaced, it is vitally important that you develop your management skills (i.e. managing your time, tracking expenses, using a planner, asking for help, etc.).

   Most people self-sabotage in this area because they assume they will understand how to handle their new increase, but they seldom do. For example, if you are accustomed to spending 40 percent of your money at your old income level, can you afford to spend 40 percent at your new level? You may be making more money, but your percentages will change, and this will directly affect you and your family.

   Learn whatever management skills are necessary to keep you where you are going ***before you get there***. In short, develop those skills out of faith that your vision will come to pass.

2. **Learn to delegate.** Your new level of success allows you to help more people, so you can't stay where you were, doing what you used to do. You must delegate.

   Most people get excited when they think about letting someone else do what they normally do, but strangely, there are things we do that we have attached value to that we are not willing to give up. Just remember that you aren't less

   > Successful people know how to delegate.

valuable because you no longer do what you used to do.

What's more, inviting people into your life to bring your success to the next level will expose weaknesses in your own life. They will see things in you that you don't want to be seen, but it's okay. You have to admit that you don't have all the strengths in the world.

In delegation, learn to pick the right people. Be critical of their skill level. You will let some people go. As you maintain the other-person focus, challenge them to reach the next level as well. Help them achieve a goal that is bigger than both of you.

Lastly, a small level of success means that you need to be good at virtually everything, but a greater level of success means that you only need to be very good at the few things you do. Delegation frees you to reach that next level.

3. **Accept that you will be perceived differently.** If you move from middle class to upper class, people will perceive you differently. The perception of the wealthy is that they are greedy, cruel, money-hungry, etc., but reality is that they probably worked harder than those who are criticizing them.

   Prepare yourself in advance for your success. Everything will change and people will make comments. You must be secure enough to know that their comments have no reality in your life, but you cannot be so hard-hearted that you lose your focus. The answer: have a soft heart and thick skin.

   Recognize that those who are positioning themselves against you are the ones who need help. Show compassion, don't get offended, and learn how to grow in your perception of self. Be humble and confident. Again, if they are family, don't cut them off. Be patient, but don't allow them to keep you at their level.

As you change, have the confidence that your changing may challenge others. You are building a legacy of doing the right thing with integrity. Rest assured, it will serve you well in the long run!

4. **Allow no negatives into your equation.** As you are trying to reach the next level, don't listen to the negatives that will be coming naturally from your comfort zone. You aren't an expert yet on your next level of success, so don't let the negatives from your comfort zone mess you up. Negatives are not "wisdom" or "being practical" or "there to stop you from making mistakes." Settle in your heart that you would rather have a disaster than never try.

> Accept that with success you will be perceived differently. (Get used to it!)

You must move forward if you are going to operate in your commandment of success. Don't let any negatives slow you down, much less keep you from trying. The commandment is that you ***must be*** successful. It will fuel you to keep going. Don't go into it thinking you ***might*** succeed. Allow no negatives.

The absence of negatives allows you to be free to try, and that puts you in the zone.

A week in the zone

What does it to take to stay in the zone all week long? It's entirely possible to stay in the zone for an entire week, then an entire month, and then an entire year. Here is how:

Massive action Monday

Go after it. The more you put into it, the more you can get out of it. Most people can succeed at a high level—they have what it takes—but they don't have massive action. The tendency is to repeat the little action that they are happy with but that gets little results. You don't have to do anything different to reap great results. It's just doing more of what works, and this is what works:

1. **Fill yourself up with massive visualization and affirmation.** People fail on this one mostly. They start the week without taking the time to figure out what they want that week. They don't say it or visualize it. The goals need to be high and challenging.

   Put your massive action to the test. Visualize and affirm. Step further than ever before. Tell yourself, "This is going to be the greatest week in my life!" Visualize winning an award. Provide yourself with a trophy at the end of the week. Get a goal and aim for it. A massive action affirmation will help you.

2. **Plan a schedule that matches your affirmation and visualization.** Set the pace for the rest of the week. Get aggressive, then make a commitment and sign it. A commitment to yourself is stronger than to anyone else. You can't cheat! If you do, you'll never grow or know if you are getting better. Massive action requires commitment.

3. **Do everything with momentum in mind.** You are preparing everything for the rest of the week. Don't let anyone steal your momentum. Build it strong because you will live off the momentum that you set on Monday. Work harder and smarter than ever before. Visualize, affirm, and then go do it!

Tuesday in the Zone!

Getting in the flow. You need to string the days together. Don't slow down after a great day on Monday.

1. **Reflect on Monday's affirmations and visualizations.** Flip back and flip forward. Every goal has an emotion attached to it. Tap the emotion. Reflect not only on Monday's affirmations and visualizations, but allow yourself to feel the results of being in the zone on Monday. The zone is first experienced emotionally. Getting in there is tapping into how you see yourself.

2. **Tell yourself, "I'm unstoppable this week!"** Push yourself to not allow anyone or anything to slow your momentum. You are building on the action of Monday. We are confident, unstoppable, and pumped. Nobody can stop you.

3. **Fill the pipeline.** The action from Monday fills the pipeline today. The pipeline is whatever you need to succeed. All you will accomplish has a pipeline. You fill it up even though you don't see results right away. Apply pressure and eventually it will pop out the other end. This will prepare you for the coming days.

Winning Wednesday

Stringing together a few good days helps you shine.

1. **Take advantage of momentum.** This is not simply the middle of the week—this is the peak. You are not going through the motions; you have purpose. You might even have to play catch-up because of your previous momentum.

2. **Don't let anyone slow you down or steal your momentum.** Invalidators will come, but don't give them time. Keep your momentum. Stay in the flow.

3. **Create a new plan of action at the end of the day for Thursday and Friday.** That new plan is based on the momentum of the week. Raise expectations for the last part of the week. Ride the wave of your week. Go over your goals. Use your affirmations and visualizations. Push yourself!

Thoroughbred Thursday

Build momentum and finish strong, just like a thoroughbred.

1. **Remind yourself that you always finish strong.** You are in shape. You are a fourth quarter person. You aren't trying to regain momentum. Instead, you are beginning to reap the benefits of filling the pipeline on Monday and Tuesday. You need to be able to receive at this time. Whatever you

> Start fast, finish strong. That is the secret to a week in the zone.

sowed, you will reap. Allow yourself to receive. Open yourself up to receive. Believe that people love you and want to bless you.

2. **If you are behind on your goals, catch up.** If you are ahead, dig in and go for more. Don't live down to your expectations. If you are behind, it's natural to push it. If you are ahead, push harder. Raise your expectations higher. Build and take yourself to new levels. Produce more than ever before.

3. **Be healthy.** Eat well, sleep well, dream well, and wake up well. It's not time to take a three-day weekend. Friday is too good to miss it. Be careful also to take care of your body.

Fortune Friday

You are worthy of the fortune. You have produced something of great value. High performance people stay in the zone till their goal is achieved.

1. **Posture everyone as if you don't need this day.** Posture—seeing yourself as you really are—is vitally important. Others see it when you see it and act it out. Think, walk, and talk as if you are the millionaire that you really are.

2. **Rejoice in every victory!** Don't let any rejection bring you down. You've had a great week. You have an attitude that you don't need anything. Don't even pause at the negative things that someone might say.

3. **Review your weekly goals.** Grade yourself. How did you do? Did you skip something to mess up

your momentum? Did you wake up feeling like a million? Claim it as if you own it. And in the last hour of the day, plan where you are going to dinner to celebrate your week in the zone.

4. **This is the time to give thanks**. There is no such thing as a self-made man.

Chapter Eight

Steps to Success

- ❒ Developing a purpose bigger than self expands your self-image. Although this can be overwhelming at first, it will one day serve you when you get tempted to do the most selfish thing a person can do—quit.

- ❒ **Reminding yourself and holding yourself accountable to being a person of destiny is key to your self-esteem. Remember in order to estimate the true value of your life vision you must keep the blueprint bright in your mind.**

- ❒ If you don't recognize your potential you will suffer from lack of desire. If a hundred dollar bill is lying on the floor in front of me, my desire level to reach for it is higher than if it is taped to the top of the space needle. Why? Because my potential level is higher. Never lose sight of your potential and you will never lack desire.

- ❒ Remember whatever you focus on you will hit. Fear and guilt and many other feelings are natural for all of us to experience when we are trying to reach higher. But don't allow yourself to dwell on these for too long or you will hit *them* rather than your goals.

- ❒ Most people simply don't allow themselves to be successful. Here is a great exercise: the next time you are thinking about doing something beyond your comfort zone, talk and think and listen to only the "why you can do it!" for one week. You will find this much harder than you think. But on the second day you will start believing and by week's end you will know how to get started.

Chapter Nine

21 wealth-building megathoughts —*Choosing the right mind-set with the right words*

It is your mind-set that will set you free. You already know it can hold you back as well as propel you forward, and that is where you are…***ready to be launched to the next level.***

Keep moving up. Don't stop. Close the back door. Keep your mind-set strong.

Affirmations that will get you there

The words that we continually feed our minds are the very words that create the pictures that, as you know, go on to form our belief systems.

To be able to move continually up from one level of success to the next, ***our words must be in sync with our vision.*** We need affirmations that support what it is we want to become and where it is we want to go.

The following twenty-one megathoughts come from ancient proverbs that I have put into today's success language. Remember that any great thought becomes that much stronger when you use the power of affirmation to take ownership over it.

#1—*Falling behind the times and becoming set in your ways will cause poverty to come on you like a thief and scarcity to become your partner.*

One of the most dangerous things about success is that what got you there might not be what keeps you there. The principles you live by might be unchanging, but the world around you isn't.

Have you ever looked into the refrigerator and what you were looking for was right in front of your face but you couldn't see it? This blind spot happens because you were expecting to see it somewhere else.

Be careful with success and don't always expect it to come from the same place or in the same timing. Keep up to date at all cost and never get set in your ways.

AFFIRMATIONS

- I am a cutting-edge thinker, always diligent to be ahead of the curve.
- I have the awesome ability to see into the future.
- (your own) ____________________________________

____

____

____

____

#2—*Many things cause anxiety and stress, but the invalidation of someone close is even more challenging to your mind-set.*

What is the greatest challenge any person committed to the next level of their success will face? The answer: the people closest to them.

Why can this be such a great challenge? First, because people close to you don't want to see you get hurt even more than they want to see you succeed. Most family and close friends naturally take a guardian roll instead of a co-visionary roll. To save you from danger they try to focus in on your weakness to help you see why you should not move forward.

If they are loved ones, don't get mad, just understand why they are highlighting your weakness. Then invite them to help you with your vision and you will see them shift from guardian to vision partner right before your eyes.

Second, beware of insecure people close to you. These people have to pull you down because they see your progress as an attack on their self-esteem. You don't have to get rid of these negative people, just hold to your vision and it will shake them loose for you. If they choose to leave your life, always remember you did not leave them, as they will try to convince you. They left you by not supporting your vision.

AFFIRMATIONS

- I validate people around me with vision.

- My vision attracts the right people and repels the wrong people from my life.

- (your own) ______________________________

____

____

____

____

#3—*Like a sniper who wounds innocent people at random is the businessperson who hires people with questionable integrity or doesn't know their background.*

Good relationships and partnerships are so hard to come by that it is easy to get into a relationship-needing mode. This is a form of a poverty mind-set. There is a big difference between reaching out to people to give them a hand up and letting people take advantage of you because you are afraid to say "no" for fear of rejection.

The wrong people in your life or business can not only have great impact on your future, but they also may act as a blockade to keep future key people from entering your life and vision. To maintain their manipulation in your life, they will always be on the lookout to block people who would make a perfect vision partner and friend. These leeches will work overtime to protect their investment of manipulation.

AFFIRMATIONS

- I am a person of great discernment of character.
- I have relationship prosperity.
- (your own) ______________________________

____

____

____

____

____

#4—*Integrity builds a healthy business and home and diversification acts as the bearing walls of your structure. Integrity + Diversification = Synergy. The high-performance person then looks to duplicate this in others, which in turn creates multiplied wealth.*

As you diversify, not only does this provide safety, but if done wisely your investments might feed and support each other. This is the foundation of synergy. The reason integrity is such a high priority to the person committed to success is that it creates a duplicable process.

Achieving a successful venture brings only limited financial gain, but when that success has been achieved in a manner that is duplicable, the wealth potential becomes multiplied. Someone once asked me, "Don't you lose your focus being so diversified?"

"Not at all," I responded, "diversification is my focus!"

AFFIRMATIONS

- I am a synergistic person.
- I am a person of high integrity and am able to see opportunities to duplicate success.
- (your own) ______________________________

____

____

____

____

#5—*Those who discipline themselves to see things in a positive light will attract positive people. But negative people are drawn to those who always see the negative side of things.*

Seeing things in a positive light is probably the greatest sign of a healthy self-esteem. Being cynical is always a big temptation because the cynic has one luxury: eventually being proven right. That is because if you predict someone else's failure long enough you will one day be proven right. I have never met a person yet who hasn't failed.

Always remember that you can be completely right and completely wrong at the same time. It's an issue of attitude. If my wife asks me if her hair looks terrible today, she is not looking for a factual answer is she? She is looking for something deeper (an affirming response). Does that mean I lie to her? No! It simply means I answer with positive insight.

AFFIRMATIONS:

- My high self-esteem causes me to see everything in a positive light.
- My positive view affects everything I do positively.
- (your own) ______________________________

____

____

____

____

#6—*When other-focused leaders prosper, their communities develop a winning attitude. But community support will turn against the self-serving leader or business.*

There is great value in gaining the support of your community. Creating win-win opportunities are the building blocks for this partnership. In accomplishing this, there are three things to remember.

1. Have a strategy to tell your own story. If you don't, a competitor might define you.
2. Do not support leaders who promote class warfare.
3. Make a commitment to have thick skin and a soft heart. Remember that leaders rarely get treated as well as they treat others. Knowing that what you are doing will ultimately serve your community can sometimes be a lonely conviction. So suck it up and simply outlast your critics!

AFFIRMATIONS

- I am an other-focused leader and people support the direction I'm going.
- I am a dynamic leader who always creates opportunities to partnership.
- (your own) ________________________________

____

____

____

____

#7—*Any vision held long enough and accurately enough will always become reality. But the person who trades a true vision for a fantasy will always get sidetracked and success will always be just out of reach.*

There is nothing wrong with having big dreams. The problem comes when you are not willing to commit to a course of action comparable to your desired end result.

The journey to success is equally as important to the fulfillment of your goal. On the way there you are learning your vision's true value. You are growing though the struggle and it is this very growth that will help you live empowered in your next level of success. Take the personal growth out and you have a fantasy, which even if somehow it can be attained, can never be maintained. A lottery ticket is the purchase of a fantasy, which can give us temporary relief from our current reality. (Sounds like a drug, doesn't it?) The statistics show that most major lottery winners lose their money in a very short period of time. Some are even destroyed by it, not because money is evil and out to destroy innocent people, but because money does not equal success.

AFFIRMATIONS

- My success is the journey.
- I am an expert in maintaining and building on my success.
- (your own) ______________________________

____

____

____

#8—*If you correct a mocker, you invite insult; if you challenge someone with no integrity, you invite abuse; if you challenge a mocker, you will be hated. On the other hand, if you correct wise people, they will be committed to you; if you mentor wise people, they will grow even wiser; if you teach people of integrity, they will increase their mind-set of success.*

The first thing I learned about creating wealth was the law of synergy: all wealth comes out of people and to tap into great wealth you must become a master of tapping into people.

This principle of wealth shows the mind-set of synergy stealers: they are committed to their low self-esteem and they can only interpret a correction as a put-down, so they respond to everything with a fight to protect themselves. Keep in mind that your words and actions are communicating to both the wise (those that see your value) and the unwise (those who don't see your value). Take note of how they respond.

It is not just talented people you are looking to partner with. Also look for people committed to personal and professional growth that put a demand on your energy, because they hold the most valued commodity of all: ***a person you can synergize with.***

Synergy is where two people come together with a level of talents and resources and the outcome isn't just double—it's ten times what you put in! That's where the money is found: in qualifying people to synergize with.

AFFIRMATIONS

- I am brave enough to attract and define the kind of person I can synergize with.

- I see talented people everywhere and they always recognize me!

- (your own) ______________________________

____

____

____

____

#9—*Whenever you fall short of your projected goals, don't act embarrassed or as though it doesn't matter. Take responsibility and get some coaching from someone who believes that you have everything it takes to win.*

The only problem that I can see with goal setting is that it draws a line in the sand. One foot short and you failed, one foot over and you are a smashing success. But we know you can't get anywhere without a goal.

One of the bravest things a person can do is to set goals. Add the following to your goals:

1. Hold your head high even if you fall short. Most people may never experience the failure you do because they are attempting a high jump with the bar set six inches off the ground! And they will never set any world records!
2. Never minimize the goal if you miss it. Although you might need to redefine it, don't back away from your desire to have that goal achieved. You simply need help with your effectiveness.
3. Accept more help as you become more successful. One of the biggest mistakes people make is being too proud to ask for help. I knew a young man who was twenty thousand dollars in debt and descending rapidly. Because his father is a friend of mine, I offered to connect a financial expert with the son at no charge. The dad was too proud and turned me down. He didn't realize that the more wealth you create, the more help—not less—you need to manage it. The same is true with goal

setting. The bigger the goals, the better the team of people you need to work with.

Affirmations

- I'm highly skilled at both setting and achieving my goals.
- I am strong enough to attract and listen to people who are experts in their field.
- (your own) ______________________________

____

____

____

____

#10—*A person that has good self-esteem can avoid arguing. But every fool is quick to quarrel. An unfocused person does not invest in the right season and when returns come in they always just miss their opportunity to reap.*

A smart person will often trade being right for the opportunity to succeed. The greatest attribute of a strong self-esteem is that it allows other people the chance to be experts.

Successful high-performance people will tell you that it is the smart people around them that got them where they are. The only time to argue through an idea is when you are cross-examining an idea to make sure it is sound, not proving who is right. Low self-esteem can cause us to lose focus of the goal and be more interested in not looking bad. It hoards rather than invests.

AFFIRMATIONS

- My strong self-esteem attracts the experts I need to fulfill my goals.
- I constantly see success as more important than being right.
- (your own) ______________________________

____
____
____
____

#11—*If your mind-set is poor, luxury will destroy you. If you see yourself as lower class, winning the lottery or quick success would cause you to self-sabotage.*

The human mind is both our greatest blessing and our greatest curse. The subconscious mind works like a thermostat—you program it for whatever degree of success and it goes to work to keep you within a few degrees of that setting.

If you get a little below your comfort zone it works overtime to get you right back up to normal. If you get a little above your comfort zone it works overtime to self-sabotage and bring you right back down to normal.

Don't get mad at yourself! You're not stupid. You just have the wrong setting programmed into your subconscious. (And don't get mad at others either; that will just lower your self-determination and cause the thermostat to get set even lower.)

AFFIRMATIONS

- I am more valuable than things; I have things, things don't have me.

- I am tremendously wealthy and make high performance decisions.

- (your own) ______________________________

____

____

____

____

#12—*Wealth quickly gained in the beginning can lose its momentum at the end.*

Most opportunities have a cycle to their success. Just look at the stock market. If you have a great month or year, don't live it up. Take that money and reinvest it so that you are guaranteed another cycle of success.

I don't believe that we should live like the bottom could fall out tomorrow—that is poverty thinking. However, we should not get lazy and assume that everything is always going to be easy and go our way. High-performance people know how to play when they are up or down, but they always play to win.

AFFIRMATIONS

- I am incredibly focused over the long haul.
- I'm like a pit bull; when I latch on to my vision, I can't be shaken off.
- (your own) ______________________________

____

____

____

____

#13—*Only manipulators think everyone is out to get them. A person of integrity has nothing to hide and responds to the future with focus and boldness.*

There are perceived quick gains that accompany manipulation. If you go down that path you will develop a mind-set that everyone is just like you and out to do the same. Totally convinced you are right, this will cause you to go into protection mode and greatly affect your positive outlook on the future.

A positive outlook is any successful person's best friend—it gets you up when others sleep in, it motivates you to get back up on that horse when most say they have had enough, etc.

People of integrity believe wholeheartedly that they deserve success. Manipulators really don't believe in success; they believe that some just cheat better than others. (This is why class warfare resonates with so many cheaters.)

AFFIRMATIONS

- I am a person of exceptional integrity and boldly pursue the next level of my success.

- I always treat others with respect and am respected in return.

- (your own) ______________________________

____

____

____

____

#14—*Successful people prioritize wisdom, they do whatever it takes to gain understanding, and they know that wisdom yields higher profits than silver or gold. Nothing you desire can compare to wisdom, which brings long life, riches, and respect.*

The mistake most people make in pursuing success is to get caught up in chasing money. To truly become successful, we have to get money chasing us. All wealth is created from within. Even a simple job is using the equation of energy in exchange for money. Increase your internal value (wisdom) and you in turn increase your personal exchange rate.

If we use everything as an opportunity for personal growth, we turn every circumstance—good or bad—into a strategy to develop wisdom, and our internal value continues to rise even in difficult times. This attitude is the foundation for a healthy stress-managed life. When people can't make sense of negative circumstances, their stress level rapidly climbs.

Stress has been said to be the number one killer. You can defeat that killer by seeing the big picture through the eyes of wisdom. Remember that it's not true success if you're not healthy and happy and can no longer enjoy it.

AFFIRMATIONS

- I see opportunity in every circumstance for personal growth.
- I never fail—I'm just one step closer to my dreams.

- (your own) ______________________________

____

____

____

____

#15—*Successful people are committed to personal growth. Unsuccessful people are too busy trying to impress others that they never learn anything. The wealth of the successful always produces security. The poverty mind-set of the unsuccessful causes them to fall prey to schemes and scams.*

The poverty mind-set manifests itself in many ways. It is always in a hurry to get money and in turn looks to opportunities it would normally never trust. It promotes a willingness to give personal power to someone else in exchange for the promise of security.

The welfare system of today has promoted dependency in the name of caring. Social security has become a joke and is expected to be bankrupt in the near future. When you are in need, your words and heart betray you by communicating selfishness…and that will never attract successful people into your life.

AFFIRMATIONS

- My creativity and work ethic is my security.
- The words I speak act like a magnet to attract the right investments and partnerships.
- (your own) ______________________________

____

____

____

____

#16—*Procrastination will make a person poor, but diligent people will eventually produce wealth.*

The root cause of procrastination is the fear of failure. None of us like to fail in front of others, especially loved ones. But we need to separate failing from being a failure.

A good friend of mine was a world-class body builder and explained that in order to build his championship physique he worked his muscle to the point of failure. By doing this, he was tearing the muscle down. Then, with proper rest and nutrition, the muscle would come back bigger and stronger than ever.

You see, failure in his vocabulary was positive, not negative. Staying proactive may cause you to fail in front of others on occasion, but it will never allow you to be defined as a failure.

Affirmations

- Temporary setbacks always prepare me for my greatest comebacks.
- I am world class at being diligent.
- (your own) ________________________________

____
____
____
____

#17—*Ill-gotten wealth has no real value. But integrity can dig you out of any hole.*

If you take away all the money from truly wealthy people, you would find that it would not be long before they had wealth again. They understand that it is not the money that makes them wealthy—***true value and true wealth come from within***.

The poverty mind-set uses money to prove to others how valuable they are. This mind-set eventually causes a lack of integrity because it cares more about image than substance. And if anything ever goes bad, it has no principle to dig its way out with.

We can't control every bad thing that happens to us, but we can control how we respond.

AFFIRMATIONS

- I am prosperous regardless of the state of the economy.
- I am wealthy within.
- (your own) ______________________________________

____

____

____

____.

#18—*A considerate man benefits himself, but an insensitive man brings trouble on himself.*

Who would you rather deal with, a person who shows you respect and kindness or someone who is impolite and discourteous? Because everyone appreciates thoughtfulness, you will find you and your ideas are much better received when you are considerate to others.

Remember that you are trying to develop long-term, trusting relationships to help you build wealth. Don't sabotage your efforts by being inconsiderate. Besides, it doesn't take any more time to be nice to people than it does to be rude.

Affirmations

- People like me and enjoy being around me because I am a compassionate and caring person.
- I am always considerate, thinking of others first.
- (your own) ______________________________

____

____

____

____

____

#19—*He who works his land will have abundant food, but he who chases fantasies lacks judgment.*

Hard (smart) work produces results, while pie-in-the-sky get-rich-quick schemes waste time and undermine self-confidence.

People who are always chasing after rainbows get disappointed over and over again. Eventually this pattern of recurring failure leads to cynicism and the belief that "nothing ever works for me." In reality, it is not the person who has been unsuccessful, but rather the plan was inferior and doomed from the start.

This isn't to say that you should be afraid to try something new, but make sure the plan is sound. If an endeavor sounds too good to be true, it usually is.

AFFIRMATIONS

- I see setbacks as opportunities to learn and a step in the right direction.
- I am fearless in going after my plans because I have solid, well-thought-out plans.
- (your own) ______________________________

____
____
____
____

#20—*The sluggard craves and gets nothing, but the desires of the diligent are fully satisfied.*

Everybody has desires, needs, and wants, but that doesn't mean anything if you are not willing to work for them. The capacity to want things has no intrinsic value in itself. We are born with desire (anyone who has had children knows that infants want something right out of the womb). Having desire is an important first step, but without hard, smart work, nothing comes to pass.

That is why it is important to spend time thinking about your desires, then making a plan to reach your goals. A useful aid to help you achieve your goals is to turn wants into needs. If you can condition your subconscious mind to really need something, then there is almost no limit to what you can accomplish. Why do you think car dealers want you to test-drive your dream car? They want you to think, "I need this car. I can't put up with my old one for another mile." If they're successful, you just bought your car.

AFFIRMATIONS

- Because I know what I need, I get what I need.
- I work hard and smart toward my goals.
- (your own) ______________________________
  ____
  ____
  ____

#21—*Do not withhold good from those who deserve it when it is in your power to act.*

Don't try to skimp and cut corners when dealing with those who contribute to your success. Pay your employees well and your bills on time. You will find that in the long run it is your relationships, both personal and business, that make you a powerful person.

Reward those who support you and they will look for ways to help make you a success.

AFFIRMATIONS

- I am surrounded by people who want to see me succeed because I am generous and considerate of others.
- I take great care of my personal and business relationships.
- (your own) ______________________________

____

____

____

____

Take these affirmations, including the ones that you write, and repeat them over and over until your sub-conscious mind believes them to be true.

Then it will be impossible for you to self-sabotage as you move from one level of success to the next!

Reference Section

EMPOWERED: How To Bring Your Dreams To Pass

Too many people settle for too little of the potential that is within them. The key to your success is staying motivated through difficult times. Learn how to keep yourself focused, prioritized, and motivated as you turn any obstacle into a valuable commodity. Six audiocassettes with three companion videos: $250

The Entrepreneur: Visualize Your Way to the Top

Learn how to visualize where you want to be—your business, your family, and your lifestyle. Set your marvelous mind to work on your goals through visualization. You will be astonished by the results! This series contains Survival Tips for the Entrepreneur and The Power of Visualization (an interview with Texas Longhorns' Coach Fred Akers). Four sessions on video and audiocassette: $200

Breaking the Barriers of Fear and Stress

In *Breaking the Barriers of Fear and Stress*, Coach Mike brings you practical tools for overcoming your fears and mastering stress. Make stress work for you! Break through the barriers in your life that prevent you from reaching your true potential. You can overcome and succeed in every aspect of your life! Four sessions on video and audiocassette: $200

Advance Leadership

The purpose of leadership is to help other people get from one place to another. The most successful leaders are those who are first willing and able to go there themselves. All of us, especially those who care about being effective leaders, need to learn to live from the inside out. In other words, we must learn to live according to our visions and goals instead of simply by responding to whatever comes our way. This series will help you to better define your role and hone your skills as a leader. Includes the Seven Laws of Affirmations and Visualization. Seven sessions on video, audio, CD and workbook: $225

Notes